Financial Planning Models

Advanced Management and Accounting Series

Series Editor: David Otley

Other titles in the series

Standard Costing
COLIN DRURY

Business Unit and Divisional Performance Measurement
MAHMOUD EZZAMEL

Capital Investment Decision-Making
DERYL NORTHCOTT

Accounting for Marketing
R. M. S. WILSON

The Social and Organisational Context of Management Accounting
A. G. PUXTY

Transfer Pricing
CLIVE EMMANUEL & MESSAOUD MEHAFDI

Overhead Cost
JOHN INNES & FALCONER MITCHELL

Information Systems for Management
DICK WHIDDETT

Principal and Agent Theory in Accounting
ANDREW STARK

Financial Planning Models

Construction and Use

G. ROLAND KAYE
The Open Business School
The Open University
Milton Keynes, UK

CIMA

Published in association with
The Chartered Institute of Management Accountants

ACADEMIC PRESS
Harcourt Brace & Company, Publishers
London San Diego New York
Boston Sydney Tokyo Toronto

ACADEMIC PRESS LTD.
24/28 Oval Road,
London NW1 7DX

United States Edition published by
ACADEMIC PRESS INC.
San Diego, California 92101–4311

This book is printed on acid-free paper

A catalogue record for this book is available from the British Library

ISBN 0–12–403770–4

Typeset by Photo·graphics, Honiton, Devon
Printed and bound in Great Britain by Mackays of Chatham plc, Chatham, Kent

Series Editor's Preface

David Otley
KPMG Peat Marwick Professor of Accounting
Lancaster University

A major problem for the management accounting teacher has been the selection of a suitable text for advanced courses. Although a number of very good texts exist, they typically do not include some topics that individual teachers wish to teach. On the other hand, they do include a considerable amount of material on topics that are unnecessary for a particular course. Students often feel that they have a poor deal in purchasing large and expensive texts that do not cover the whole of their course, yet include large amounts of extraneous material.

This series is an attempt to resolve this problem. It will consist of a set of slim volumes, each of which deals with a single topic in depth. A coherent course of study may therefore be built up by selecting just those topics which an individual course requires, so that the student has a tailor-made text for the precise course that is being taken. The texts are aimed primarily at final year undergraduate courses in accounting and finance, although many will be suitable for MBA and other postgraduate programmes. A typical final year advanced management accounting option course could be built around four or five texts, as each has been designed to incorporate material that would be taught over a period of a few weeks. Alternatively, the texts can be used to supplement a larger and more general textbook.

Each text is a free-standing treatment of a specific topic by an authoritative author. They can be used quite independently of each other, although it is assumed that an introductory or intermediate-level management accounting course has been previously taken. However, considerable care has been taken in the choice and specification of topics, to ensure that the texts mesh together without unnecessary overlap. It is therefore hoped that the series will provide a valuable resource for management accounting teachers, enabling them to design courses that meet precise needs whilst still being able to recommend required texts at an affordable price.

Preface

Financial Planning is an essential activity for both the individual and corporate survival. The development of computer-assisted planning tools permits the exploration of a greater range of futures. This predictive power enables us to influence our own future. This is a powerful tool in a volatile economic climate.

We now take for granted the availability of Personal Computers with easily controlled spreadsheets and beautifully presented reports incorporating text tables and graphics to highlight key issues. However the ease of the report generation and our subjective belief in the truth of the printed word may mask a deeper uncertainty in the quality of the data and the legitimacy of the evidence. We are now in the realms of computer assisted bankruptcy, where our model's complexity (measured in megabytes) is greater than our mental ability to conceptualise and validate informally. There is a need to develop formal methods of building, testing and implementing, models. This book seeks to assist the reader in developing valid and reliable financial planning models.

Model Building is not technology dependent but enabled through it. Technology has the power to overrun its user and so the emphasis in the text is on building models in the mind and on paper as well. This discipline ensures learning and testing as well as the maintenance of essential documentation for auditing and validating the products of our endeavours. The book does not concentrate on any specific technology. In fact, the approach used may be applied to most platforms, from spreadsheets to modelling systems, from mainframe to micro. Many of the illustrations in the book have been built and tested across a number of platforms. Comments on the weaknesses of generic systems are cautions to the reader. These do not imply criticism of any specific packages but rather limitations for which the user must allow.

This book reflects a number of years teaching and research of management accounting with computers. In writing this text I found difficulty in deciding what to exclude. This reflects the teaching and consultancy experience where students and delegates have sought to include more in the programmes than time will allow. An explanation for this is the charisma of model building, the control of their model and technology, the joy of generating a prediction. Modelling is a powerful learning device that allows the modeller to explore their understanding, testing beliefs and developing new enquiries. It represents a forum into which our understanding of accounting and finance may be explored and challenged. The underlying economic relationships expressed mathematically can be represented and tested with empirical data. A course in modelling draws together many of the building blocks of accounting and finance. It requires implicit procedures of techniques to be made explicit algorithms for coding into the computer. This requires a formal declaration of the accounting and finance rules and relationships.

The book develops from a review of 'what is Financial Planning?', to then explore the contributions of Economics, Finance, Operations Management and Accounting to the activity of Model Building. A number of models are then explored to illustrate the type and range of applications. The text continues throughout with a large number of illustrations including diagrams and example. I hope these help the reader to relate the description to the activity of model building.

Two chapters are devoted to exploring a formal approach to model building that take the developer from problem definition through the analysis to testing and implementation. The text includes a number of examples in Management Accounting from budgeting to corporate planning, from cash flow to investment appraisal. The text concludes by examining the application of models to Decision Supports that have seen the growth of dedicated models and reporting systems. The text is intended to stimulate a desire for more information and hence references to further reading are supplied throughout.

My thanks to past delegates, students and colleagues for their contributions to this work.

Contents

1

Introduction

You may be planning to start a business, co-ordinating departmental budgets, or developing strategic plans – all these activities share a common need to develop and explore financial planning models.

Managers frequently use models to gain an insight into their business and its behaviour. Management use models in their decision making to explore the consequences of alternative choices open to them. Frequently, models supplied by the accountant owe their origin to economics, finance and operational research. The models are primarily quantitative, leaving managers to justify qualitative aspects.

Historically, accountants and managers alike performed recalculations to explore alternative choices. Now the computer performs the same recalculations in a fraction of a second. This frees the manager to explore the alternatives and to develop the model further. While recalculation can be performed more efficiently with the aid of a computer, model building and programming the computer to perform the modelling task requires a disciplined approach.

Originally, the justification for building a model was the frequency of usage to perform a number of recalculations, where the significance of the decision justified the cost. This philosophy applied in the early years of computer modelling, but recently the technology has become more readily accessible and the simplified modelling tools have become more user-friendly. With the support of personal computers and spreadsheets, managers and accountants alike have been empowered to perform their own financial planning and modelling.

DEFINITION OF FINANCIAL PLANNING

Carrying out a bibliographic search on the title "financial planning" will produce a response from a number of literature fields. The literature will come predominantly from accounting and finance, but references are found in economics and econometrics, as well as in computing. If we analyse this literature base we find that the activity of financial planning and the medium of measurement dominate, rather than the problem that is being analysed. This perhaps explains why such disparate texts as personal taxation and managerial economics can contain chapters on financial planning.

Planning is concerned primarily with developing schemes for achieving a given objective in the future. In the case of personal tax planning, the objective may be tax minimization of capital transfer. Alternatively, the treasurer may be concerned with shareholder wealth maximization in evaluating capital projects and funding decisions. For the management accountant, the objective may be efficient use of the resources of the firm within the planning period, as in budgetary control. All these planning activities can be differentiated from the planning activities of architects, production schedulers and distribution managers by the common use of financial measurement and the emphasis on the monetary resources.

Financial planning is a process of:

- analysing the interaction of financing and investment choices open to the firm;
- projecting the future consequences of present decisions in order to avoid surprises and to understand the links between present and future decisions;
- deciding which alternatives to undertake;
- measuring subsequent performance against the goals set in the financial plan.

Planning incorporates the activity of predicting the future outcomes of events. This may lead to the development of plans to cope with the predicted future events, including influencing events and the forecast. Financial planning equates with predicting the future in financial terms and/or the prediction of the future requirements for finance. Financial planning sits between the disciplines of finance and planning and uses models to represent the problem area.

The contents of a financial plan include:

1. a report which is understandable to users, probably using a pro-forma accounts layout of profit and loss account, funds flow and balance sheet (see Table 1.1 below). (NB these reports are forecasts and not historic);

2. a statement of expenditure, which identifies capital expenditure and changes in working capital;
3. a statement of revenue and financing structures and sources. This should incorporate expected income and identify additional finance required;
4. a forecast which is a prediction of future states, reflecting the alternatives under examination. The accuracy of the prediction reflects that of the model. Repeated testing, refining and improvement permit the predictive quality to rise. One hundred percent accuracy is not possible!

In addition, the financial planning process will incorporate a forum for expressing knowledge and understanding, acquired through the model-building process that is subject to testing, validation and refutation. Models and financial plans have life cycles with short-term models developing within the long-term structure of knowledge and understanding. Models are a simplification of reality and cannot replace reality.

In Example 1, we have illustrated a simple financial model in which the base year data of 1992 are used to derive results for 1993 to 1997. The performance in the forecast years is dependent on the sales forecasts that have been entered as predictions based on the estimates of growth and cyclical trends. The structure of the model cascades from the profit and loss account through the sources and application of funds to the closing balance sheet at the end of the year. The profits generated from the sales activity are used to finance the payment of dividends and taxes, while the retained profits finance the growth in both fixed assets and working capital necessary to support the sales prediction. The growth in debentures is necessary to finance the expansion that cannot be financed by retained earnings.

We shall return to this model later to examine its structure and logic. The model utilizes the financial structure of 1992 as a basis for deriving the predictions of the subsequent years. However, the reader should appreciate that the model requires the input of the sales forecast from which the prediction of the changes is generated.

EXAMPLE 1.1

Illustrative financial model

Profit and loss account £000	**Base 1992**	**Forecast 1993**	**1994**	**1995**	**1996**	**1997**
Sales	2 160	2 000	2 200	2 500	2 450	2 500
Cost of sales	1 944	1 800	1 980	2 250	2 205	2 250

Profit	216	200	220	250	245	250
Interest	36	26	34	43	41	40
EBT	180	174	186	207	204	210
Tax at 50%	90	87	93	103	102	105
Net income	90	87	93	103	102	105
Sources and applications						
Net income	90	87	93	103	102	105
Depreciation	80	74	81	93	91	93
Operating cash flow	170	161	174	196	193	198
Borrowing	0	−109	−19	190	75	−42
Stock issue	64	0	0	0	0	0
Total sources	234	52	156	386	268	156
Uses:						
Increase in WC	40	−14	5	47	23	0
Investment	140	14	95	278	183	93
Dividend	54	52	56	62	61	63
Total uses	234	52	156	386	268	156
Balance sheet						
Fixed assets	800	740	814	925	907	925
Net working capital	200	186	205	233	228	233
Capital employed	1 000	926	1 019	1 158	1 134	1 158
Financed by:						
Equity	600	635	637	676	678	718

Debentures	400	291	381	481	456	439
Total	1 000	926	1 019	1 158	1 134	1 158

PRINCIPLES OF MODELLING IN FINANCIAL PLANNING

In everyday life we apply our knowledge, experience and skills to make decisions and solve problems. Most of the time, this takes place intuitively, as a matter of routine; on other occasions there is an explicit process. In all cases there are a series of activities that we know collectively as problem solving and decision making. Both problem solving and decision making have the same route but in the case of the former there may be an absence of choice in the outcome.

Figure 1.1 shows the life cycle of a decision. This life cycle applies equally to problem solving, the only difference perhaps being that of the degree of choice. Initially we must have problem identification. This may be signalled quite clearly (e.g. What price shall we sell the new product at?), or the problem may remain hidden for some time before some symptom reveals its existence (e.g. stocks rise to the point of creating problems of storage and cash flow due to poor sales performance). The problem may exist in the real world, as illustrated by the foregoing examples, or it may be a conceptual problem, arising from our lack of

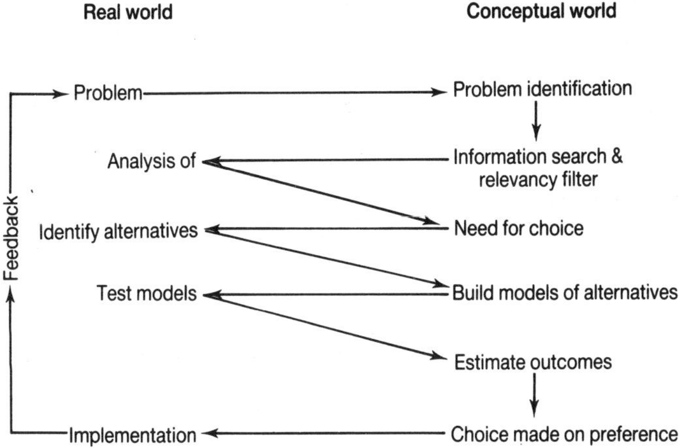

FIGURE 1.1 Life cycle of a decision

understanding of the real world. In both cases the problem will be solved only after analysis of the real world. This analysis should lead to the synthesis of ideas that we call understanding. An alternative definition of this process is modelling.

The concern of this text is the application of modelling. In particular, we are concerned with the application to financial decision-making, regarding a business. To understand the elements of the model and their interrelationships, a systems approach is used. Figure 1.2 illustrates the basic assumptions of a business system. The systems view is reflected not only in the accounting system but also in the physical flows of activity through the business. A business model will seek to represent this system. A systems model is an abstract, simulating reality by feeding in data and predicting the likely outcome. Business models are probabilistic; neither true nor false in their predictions. Their usefulness can only be established by comparing their predictions with reality; the probability of the outcome being as predicted is independent of how risk and uncertainty have been built into the model. Any abstraction of reality must have a degree of probability associated with the prediction, reflecting the degree of abstraction.

The business model also stresses the relationships between internal and external factors on the firm (Figure 1.3). This recognition of relationships is a vital ingredient in financial planning as it reflects the relationships of economics and strategic management. It should be noted that the degree of influence reduces as we move outside the firm and consequently the model must become more responsive to external factors to permit exploration of alternative courses of action.

Financial planning is concerned with the decision and control process. We find that the tools of financial planning may be applied not only to the traditional planning modes but also to the other elements of the

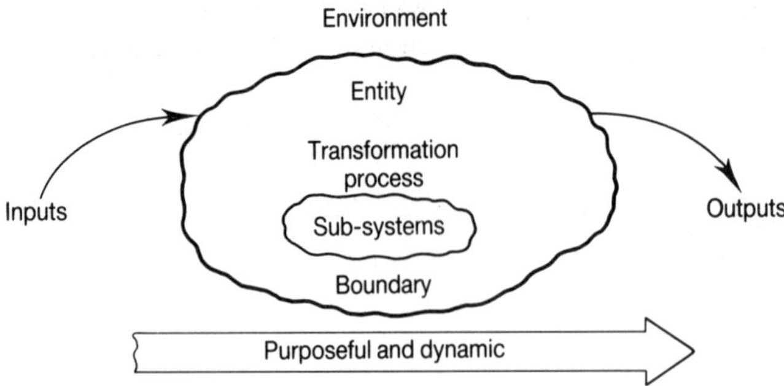

FIGURE 1.2 A business model

		Influences	
		Internal	External
Conditions of environment	Certain	Optimising	
	Uncertain		Simulation

FIGURE 1.3 Planning technique and conditions of environment

cycle. Two writers on planning theory, Faludi (1976) and Camhis (1979), both believe that this activity can be seen to have alternative philosophies. These philosophies may be represented at the extremes by the concepts of blueprint planning and disjointed incremental planning. Blueprint planning we may conceive of as a formalizing of the budget that we then use, unadjusted, as a yardstick for the whole year. Alternatively, we may represent blueprint planning as the process through which an architect designs a standard house, producing a blueprint for that new house. At the other extreme, disjointed incremental planning represents much more the operational planning on a day-to-day basis, where plans are forever being amended and adjusted in the light of experience and the need to react to circumstances. Alternatively, we may represent it by the extensions and modifications that we make to our houses. In my own case, my house was built in the 1820s and has been through five clear phases of modification. This text seeks to look at the financial planning process that covers all these extremes of philosophy. The strength of the software that we are using lies in its ability to be flexible and permit amendment and adjustment. This would naturally seem to support the disjointed incremental process but it is also useful in developing the blueprint, since blueprinting activity essentially requires a freezing at some time of the policies and elements portrayed in the budget. In this respect our planning tools permit any philosophy to be established, so organizations may continue to follow their philosophy of planning using the same planning tools as an organization following a different philosophy.

The relevance of the issue of planning process and philosophies lies in the control or planning cycle; see Figure 1.4. The planning or control cycle is the activity through which we attempt to control some activity. First, plans are established. Second, we measure outcomes and compare the outcome with the plan. The comparison results in either feedback or feed forward. Feedback is information leading to correction of the activity to bring it in line with the plan. Feed forward is information leading to pre-emptive action, such as revision of the plan.

This strengthens the view that the software is a tool while the financial planning process of model building is a problem-solving analysis that

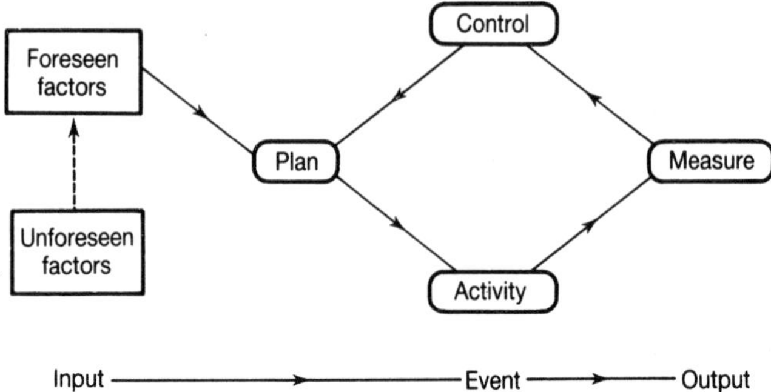

FIGURE 1.4 Planning and control loop

enables attention to be focused on the relevant factors. This process of analysis is one from which we gain insight into our business activity and for which we traditionally require experience. A way of passing on that experience and retaining it in the business is by incorporating it into the models we use for decision and control. To get there we must build more sophisticated models. To help us we can enlist operational researchers as well as building generations of models. Perhaps our basic method must be to build models that link the planning process, the reporting process, the forecasting process and the control process.

The modelling process consists of seven stages:

1. Problem definition.
2. Problem analysis.
3. Parameter estimation.
4. Specification of the model.
5. Encoding the model.
6. Testing the model.
7. Implementation.

The advantages of modelling may be summarized as follows:

- It provides a framework for examining problems. Although a model may not always lead to a solution, it is possible that it may highlight gaps in information.
- The process of building the model contributes to a better understanding of the problem.
- Models allow manipulation of both the rules and the data, to test a wide variety of possible outcomes.
- Models are easier and less expensive than carrying out full-scale exercises, saving both time and money.

- Communication between managers within a business is aided.
- A longer time horizon may be considered.
- The consistency of plans can be checked.

Users of financial modelling systems should also be aware of some of the disadvantages of modelling, which include:

- The danger of over-simplification – the model builder may leave out crucial factors for expediency.
- Symbolic language, though valuable, has its limitations, and not every relationship can be expressed mathematically.
- Model builders can become so enamoured of their models that they begin to believe they are better than reality, and the model becomes rigid.
- Models produce only predictions of outcomes. These might be simple figures (as in a budget) or a range of results with an indication of the one most likely to occur.
- Models are never (or extremely rarely) absolutely right, leading some people to perceive them as inherently inaccurate.
- The quality of data and its availability will not only affect the model's structure but also the quality of prediction.
- The output from models may be used for political purposes, leading to manipulation of assumptions to give the answers required.

TYPES OF MODEL

A model is a representation of reality. It might be a physical model, such as a model of an aircraft undergoing wind tunnel testing, or an abstract model using mathematical formulae to represent size, shape, weight, relationships, etc. The following are some descriptions of types of model.

- Iconic: looks like.
- Analog: behaves like.
- Symbolic: representative of.
- Mathematical: mathematically representative of.
- Descriptive: descriptive of behaviour, relationships, physical characteristics, etc.
- Deterministic: behaves in prescribed patterns.
- Probabilistic: behaviour only predicts probabilities.
- Static: static representation.
- Dynamic: changing representation.
- Algorithmic: optimized and structured.
- Heuristic: trial and error.

MANAGEMENT ACCOUNTING AND FINANCIAL PLANNING

Management accounting may be defined as "the provision of information" required by management for such purposes as:

- Formulation of policies.
- Planning and controlling the activities of the enterprise.
- Decision taking on alternative courses of action.
- Disclosure to those external to the entity, such as shareholders and others.
- Disclosure to employees.
- Safeguarding assets.

The process involves participation of management to ensure that:

- plans are developed to meet objectives (long-term planning);
- short-term operation plans are formulated (short-term budgeting, profit planning);
- there is recording of actual transactions, financial accounting and cost accounting;
- corrective action is taken to bring future and actual transactions into line (financial control);
- finance is obtained and controlled (treasuryship);
- there is reviewing and reporting on systems and operations (internal audit and management audit).

This summary is all-embracing of the traditional accounting functions, with perhaps the exclusion of the external audit and taxation aspect.

It is reasonable to expect that management accountants will be users of financial modelling. This will particularly apply to the formulation of strategic and long-term planning, the formulation of short-term operating plans, i.e. budgeting, and to other *ad hoc* planning and decision activities. This has been confirmed in the study by Collier (1984) which found that management accountants were active users of financial modelling tools.

The information flow starts with the implementation of the plans in the activity. The outcome of the activity is measured and the result compared with the plan. This information flow concerning actual activity is naturally historic, although real-time systems are increasingly being implemented.

In order to make this data have real meaning, we must compare the output results with the input plans – this is done in the comparison (Figure 1.5). Information may be distinguished from data, in that it has a value to the receiver and leads to action. This can be seen in the comparison stage where information generated from the comparison

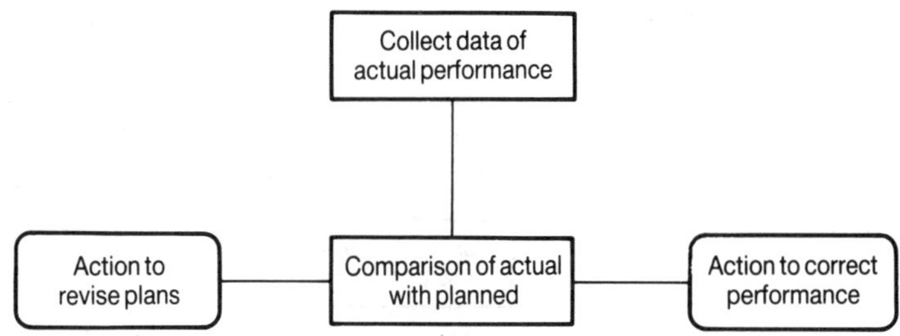

FIGURE 1.5 Control feedback model

results in either feedback (corrective action to the activity through the amendment of the future flows) or feed forward (which leads to the revision of the plans and subsequent activities).

Essentially the management accounting routines are cycles of forecasting, measuring and comparing, leading to re-forecasting and reaction to variances (Figure 1.6). These routines are the natural basis on which the computerization of management accounting and management information systems have evolved. It is only natural therefore that we should consider how organizations have achieved this in practice.

REACTING COSTS MONEY; PLANNING SAVES MONEY

The above statement summarizes the philosophy of the financial planning process. A common example of a financial plan in management accounting is the budget. The budget is a model of the organization, but like other financial plans, in isolation it is no better than an empty diary. It requires usage by implementation and review of outcomes. This integration of planning and control is vital to improvement in the quality of the plans and the planning process. CIMA defines budgetary control as 'the establishment of budgets relating the responsibilities of executives to the requirements of a policy, and the continuous comparison of actual with budgeted results, either to secure by individual action the objective of that policy or to provide a basis for its revision.'

Clearly, this definition of budgetary control, with its emphasis on responsibilities and the process of comparison, action and revision, highlights the activity as being managerial rather than accounting. With this view in mind, it is reasonable for organizations to use the budgeting process with modelling tools as an opportunity to widen the participation

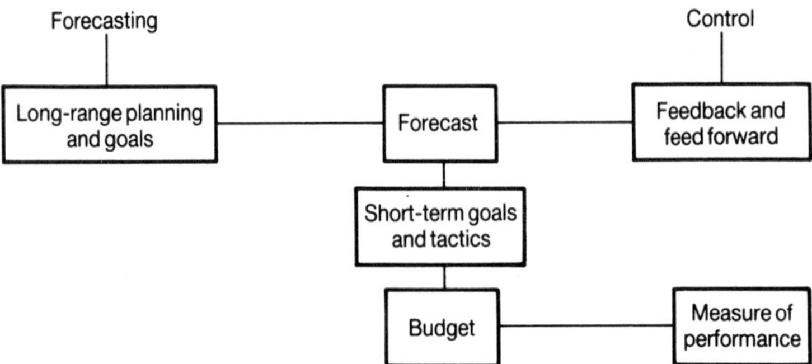

FIGURE 1.6 Interconnection of forecasting and control systems

of management in the budget process. This sentiment should be pursued with all financial models that enable communication and sharing of perceptions.

As with all models, the model that we build may be simple or complex. The simple model has the attraction of taking little effort to build and being easily understood. However, its major drawback is its potential lack of realism in reflecting the complexity of the organization, the structures and inter-connection of the organization and its environment. The behaviour of the elements within the organization is simplified. These elements contain the cost relationships and revenue behaviours as well as the capital employed elements. Also embodied are the other dimensions of the model, namely the production capacity, utilization, material availability, etc. To overcome this, the model has traditionally reduced the problems of variety by aggregation in the same way that aggregation takes place in the management accounting reports, from the detail of individual departments through to the total picture of the business as expressed in the operating statement. This principle applies in the budgeting process, where we start with a detailed look at the sales, moving through to production thence to department costs and eventually arriving at profit and loss account, balance sheet and cash flow statement.

Another way of handling this complexity is the evolution of new models from existing models as we add further complexity as our understanding increases. This is an essential ingredient of the budgeting process that requires validating or testing against the actual behaviour of the organization. This process of developing the model is enhanced by the dynamic approach to reforecasting and reformulating the budget offered by the utilization of spreadsheets and financial modelling packages.

The difference between these two processes is the inclusion of personnel, procedures, and policy making. In our description of the modelling process we assumed that people were undertaking the task using resources and making decisions along the way. There is accountability and responsibility. In the budgeting process we have always made explicit these elements, and this practice should be followed in all financial planning.

The subsequent comparison of actual with desired performance leads to action and reaction. This in turn feeds into our future world, moulding the expectations of management that will define and influence the future forecasts. This becomes, therefore, a closed loop with the addition of the dynamic modelling process.

In many organizations the budget co-ordinator and membership of the budget committee often provide a learning forum for senior personnel and those destined for senior positions. This reflects the learning potential that the analysis process provides in understanding the organization that we are seeking to manage. The principle of learning applies to all planning processes and the formal recognition and incorporation of planning into procedures and processes should be encouraged.

STRUCTURE AND OBJECTIVE OF TEXT

This text aims to provide a foundation in the principles of financial model building that may be applied to spreadsheets and modelling systems. The text aims to provide a reader with:

- an understanding of financial model building;
- an awareness of the range of techniques and types of models;
- an ability to develop and utilize financial planning models;
- an appreciation of the process of implementation on spreadsheets and modelling systems;
- a process of model building that incorporates testing and improvement.

The text assists the reader to implement theory into practice and specifically supports the user in using modelling and spreadsheets to perform financial planning activities. Experienced modellers will find the formal process of planning helpful in refining their own working practices. Financial planners will find the variety of financial models discussed in the text equally stimulating in developing more advanced models.

There are three key perspectives on financial planning that this text considers:

1. Business planning as performed through a financial model of the firm.
2. Planning of the financial resources of the firm.
3. The facilitating of the above by the application of IT.

To undertake this the text draws on the literatures of:

- accounting;
- finance;
- operations research;
- econometrics;
- computer studies.

The text assumes the underlying coverage of these disciplines as included in foundation or preliminary undergraduate courses in accounting, finance and business studies, and MBA programmes. It moves from an introductory perspective of predicting financial requirements, to considering the alternative philosophies and methods for planning as found in the business planning and control hierarchy. The alternative views of accounting, corporate finance, econometrics and operational research are critically examined to establish a common method of modelling and planning which can be married to the technology of computer modelling.

The method of modelling is examined in the context of some example models drawn from the literature that illustrate the key alternative model structures. The development of a financial planning model is then considered in a formal method as part of the life cycle of decision making and model evolution. In this context "good modelling practice" is suggested and applied to spreadsheet and modelling systems.

The text then returns to the planning hierarchy and examines the planning process and model structures developed for corporate planning, budgeting, and short-term decision making. In so doing, issues of decision supports and innovative techniques such as executive information systems are introduced. This also leads back to the application of financial plans to decision making and the consideration of individual and group decision-making behaviour.

Teaching strategy

The material in this text is based on the author's experience of teaching an option in Financial Planning and Computer Modelling to final year undergraduates and postgraduates, as well as short courses in financial modelling, and consulting with organizations on financial analysis and modelling.

To develop a competence in financial modelling and planning, experience of the analysis, development and implementation process is essential. It has been found that developing this competence is possible by bringing together practical sessions on the stages of modelling with lectures and seminars on the framework.

The development of a substantial model by students (preferably working on independent problems but sharing learning experiences) based on real life data greatly enhances the learning experience and the acquisition of practical skills. Exposure to a range of models, problem situations, data sets, and software enables the acquisition of essential experience, including critical insight into the shortcomings of different approaches.

SUMMARY

In this chapter we have laid the foundation of the text, providing an overview of the nature of financial planning and modelling, the contributing disciplines and a description of the process which will be adopted to build models and develop financial plans. We have indicated the structure and philosophy of the text and a teaching strategy which integrates the theory with the practice of model building in an organizational and managerial context.

Further reading

Anthony, R.N. (1965) *Planning and Control Systems – a framework for analysis*, Cambridge, Mass.: Harvard UP.

Asch, D. and Kaye, G.R. (1989) *Financial Planning – Modelling Methods and Techniques*, London: Kogan Page.

Bridges, J. (1989) *Managerial Decisions with the Microcomputer*, Hemel Hempstead: Philip Allan.

Bryant, J.E. (ed.) (1987) *Financial Modelling in Corporate Management* (2nd edn), Chichester: John Wiley.

Camhis, H. (1979) *Planning Theory*, London: Tavistock.

Collier, P.A. (1984) *The Impact of Information Technology on the Management Accountant*, London: ICMA.

Faludi, A. (1976) *Planning Theory*, Oxford: Pergamon.

Lee, C.F. (1985) *Financial Analysis and Planning – Theory and Application*, Wokingham: Addison Wesley.

Quinn, J.B. (1980) *Strategies For Change*, Homewood, Ill.: Irwin.

Schlosser, M. (1989) *Corporate Finance: A model building approach*, Hemel Hempstead: Prentice Hall.

Wildsmith, J.R. (1973) *Managerial Theories of the Firm*, Oxford: Martin Robertson.

2

Alternative Views of Financial Planning

INTRODUCTION

Finance is often assumed to be the natural home of financial planning. In bookshops, financial planning texts are classified under headings as diverse as taxation, accountancy, economics, mathematics and even computing. It is helpful to consider the contribution of these disciplines.

In this chapter we consider some of the influences and source disciplines that form the domain of financial planning today. The disciplines that we draw on are econometrics, finance, accounting and operational research. Each of these disciplines contains an element of financial planning and has contributed to the central area of financial planning. While financial planning may be studied in each of these respective disciplines, there are shortcomings in only considering a single perspective (Figure 2.1).

We do not intend that the reader should be given a comprehensive coverage of financial planning in these respective disciplines, but rather would encourage readers who wish to take their study further to turn to those disciplines and study in depth their contribution to financial planning.

ECONOMETRICS

Econometrics deals with the measurement of economic relationships. It is a combination of mathematical economics and statistics. Econometrics

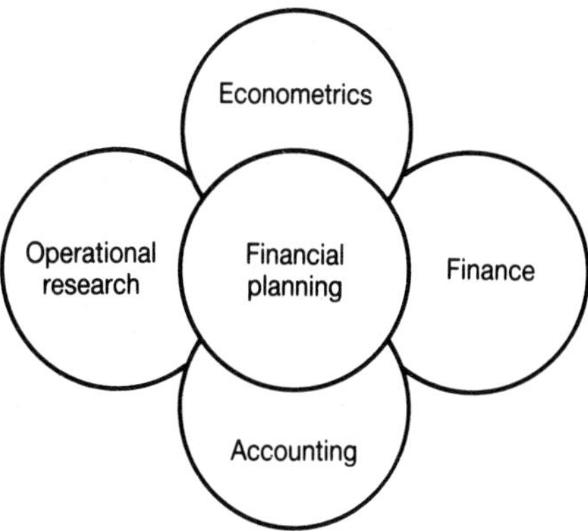

FIGURE 2.1 The overlap and shared territory of the disciplines of financial planning

is the integration of these elements to provide parameter estimation of economic relationships and the verification of economic theory. Statistics are heavily used to analyse and identify the numerical values of the parameters that form the economic relationship. In doing so, the empirical measurement of economic phenomena is drawn upon.

Economic theory postulates relationships that may be subjected to testing. Testing is performed by confronting theory with empirical data. Econometrics provides a method for confronting the theory with data that proves or rejects the theory. This activity requires the use of mathematical models to express the relationships embodied in the economic theory.

The goals of econometrics are:

1. analysis and testing of economic theory;
2. the development of policies based on numerical estimates of coefficients of economic relationships that may be used for decision making;
3. forecasting based on the estimates of coefficients in order to forecast future values of economic events.

Econometrics contributes two important perspectives to the activity of financial planning. First, it provides an economic framework for financial planning of an entity. If we are concerned with financial planning of the firm, econometrics not only provides us with models of the economic environment in which the firm trades, but also models of the marketplace for both consumption and supply of goods. Within the firm, the production function is an important idea, for understanding marginal costs and the cost drivers within the firm. Second, econometrics is based in two main categories of model: single equation techniques, in which one relationship at a time is examined – for example, the demand function; and simultaneous equations, in which multiple relationships are examined together. Simultaneity is an important element in financial modelling of concepts such as debt financing, interest rates and finance requirements within the firm.

Econometrics provides us with rigour in approaching the model building exercise, which is the basis of the financial planning process. Figure 2.2 illustrates the econometric approach to building a model that develops from a theoretical view through a model building exercise to the testing and evaluating of the theory. The objective of testing theory is refutation, rather than confirmation. Only by following this procedure is it possible to develop rigorous models that can be subject to development, reflecting our increasing understanding of real world situations, which we embody in our theories.

The model will be expressed in the form of mathematical equations. The value of these variables that form the equations will be defined either externally (exogenous) or derived from the model (endogenous). The exogenous variables include the assumptions and constants built into the model and the input variables that drive the model. The endogenous variables will include the results we seek from the model.

Econometric models may be developed by two approaches (Figure 2.3). First, *a priori*, where a model is developed from grounded theory. This may be undertaken where an explicit model structure is to be used which will be confronted with the best available data in estimating the

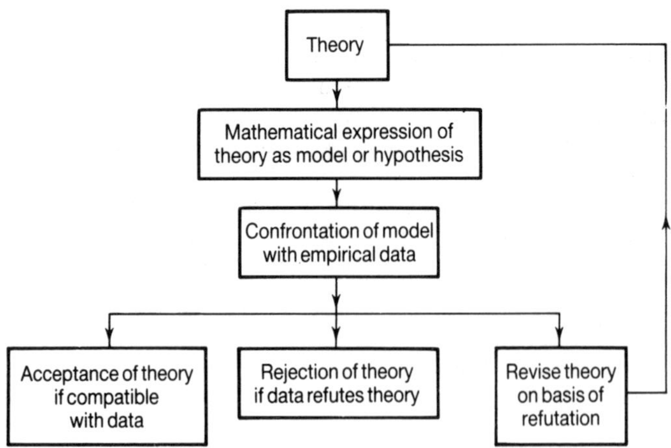

FIGURE 2.2 Econometric modelling process

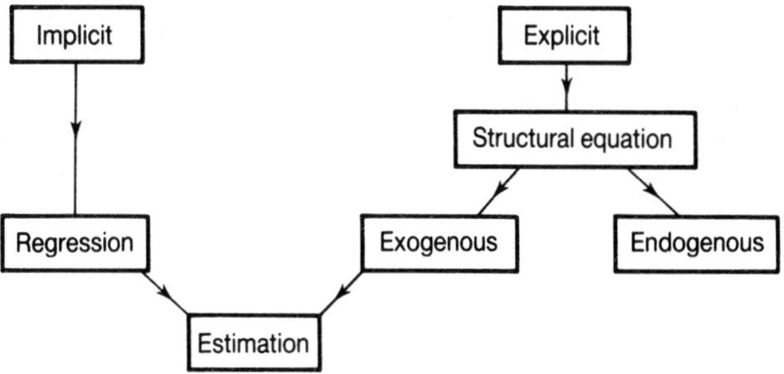

FIGURE 2.3 Alternative origins of econometric models

parameters. In this approach, the modeller would collect all available information from theory and practice of relevance to the phenomenon being studied. The modeller would then select a structural equation on an *a priori* basis. Estimation of the parameters of the model would then take place with the available data using statistical techniques of correlation, regression, tests of significance and analysis of variances.

Alternatively an experimentation approach may be adopted, whereby through a system of trial and error the implicit model is identified. The modeller will start with a simple model containing few variables and equations, but these will be revised in the light of the tests. The models are confronted with data. On the basis of the statistical evidence of the performance, additional variables are added and more complex structures adopted (including non-linear forms). This approach combines the *a priori* with empirical observation to develop models from implicit situations. If no existing theory is available or yet identified, then a process of estimation must be pursued, based on analysis of the data using regression techniques to permit the development of insight into the implicit relations in the data.

The outcomes of these estimation processes are the values of parameters within the chosen theoretical model, which may be either a single equation or simultaneous equations. The quality of the estimation is reflected in the correlation between the data and the estimate as demonstrated by the tests of significance and variance, but also in the subsequent testing of the model forecasts against future outcomes.

Econometric models should:

- be theoretically plausible;
- have an exploratory ability;
- reflect the accuracy or confidence in the estimates of parameters;
- possess a forecasting ability;
- embody simplicity and elegance.

MANAGERIAL ECONOMICS AND CORPORATE STRATEGY

An important development of econometrics has taken place in the area of managerial economics, that traditionally concentrates on demand analysis, production and cost analysis and theory of the firm within the market structure. This approach can form a very significant contribution to the theoretical underpinning of the practice of corporate and strategic planning. Although corporate planning is only one subset of financial planning and modelling, this area should not be ignored. Porter's work (1980) on corporate strategy and the competitive environment is fundamentally based on economic models of the firm, and the firm's competitive position with the market-place. Porter recognized that the competitive position of the firm was dependent not only on the rivalry between competing firms within an industry, but also on the relative balance of power between supplier and buyer in the market-place. Rivalry may be further increased by the ease of entry and exit of new competitors and the number of substitutes (Figure 2.4). Using this approach, strategic planning may be identified as a problem of portfolio management, an investment problem and a selection of strategy problems.

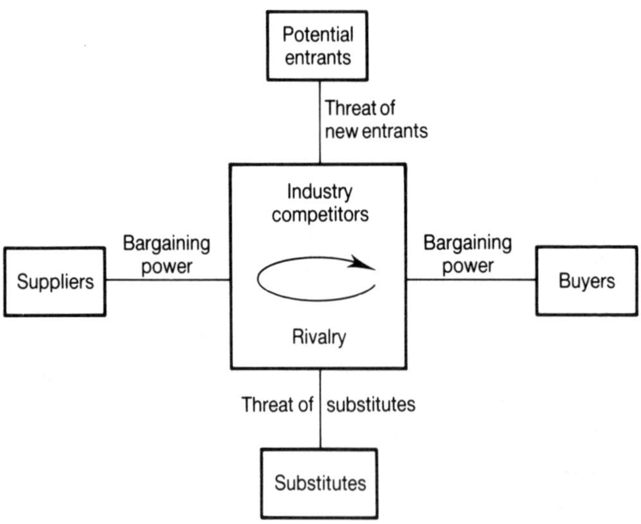

FIGURE 2.4 Five Forces
Source: Porter 1980

Essentially, strategic planning requires the management of a portfolio of investments that have been named and are being added to over time through subsequent investment. The selection of a strategy to pursue with the existing portfolio is essentially one of contraction, expansion or selection amongst the ruling expectations of the market-places in which the firm operates. The contribution of macro- and micro-economic theory to practical business problems can be seen here, and the role of econometrics in providing a method of estimating and analysing real data sets reflecting the environment in which the firm operates and the cost of operation.

FINANCE

The literature on finance suggests that financial planning is a process of:

1. Analysing the interaction of financing and investment choices open to the firm.
2. Projecting the future consequences of present decisions in order to avoid surprises and understanding the links between present and future decisions.
3. Deciding which alternatives to undertake.
4. Measuring subsequent performance against the goals set in the financial plan.

This is rather a narrow definition of financial planning, in that the primary focus is on financial resources. The management of the other resources of the firm, such as the plant and the machinery, land and buildings, working capital and personnel, are viewed as investment opportunities. It is the responsibility of managers to manage the resources effectively and efficiently to achieve the corporate goals. In order for them to act, they have to have some expectations of what will happen. The manager needs prediction – a theory about outcomes of action – built up from experience and reasoning. Managers need to consider the financial implications of their actions that lead to the financial predictions of outcomes from these actions. Financial expressions of these outcomes are required. In this way, a co-ordinated approach may be taken through the common financial measurement process. Financial planning is not just a forecast, but forecasts may form an element of the process. The process includes the analysis of the situation, the prediction of financial outcomes of alternative actions, the selection and implementation of a choice of action, and subsequent monitoring of outcome. In so doing, risk and uncertainty may be identified and attempts made to quantify them. The focus is on making informed choices based on financial predictions of alternative actions.

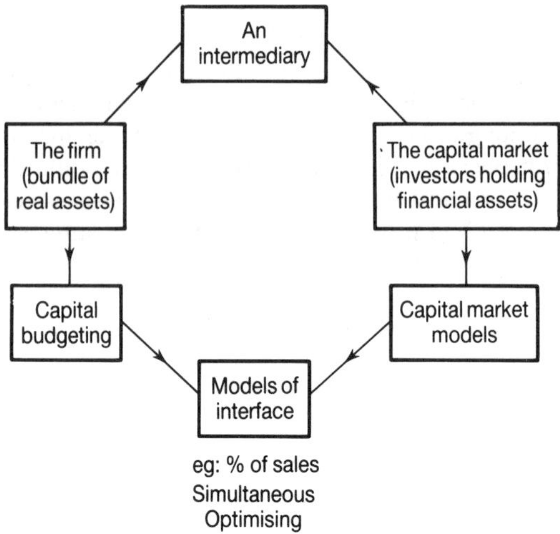

FIGURE 2.5 Financial modelling process. NB: The financial models which reflect this interface include: the percentage of sales (see Chapter 3), optimizing and simultaneous examples (see Chapter 6)

Finance has a firm foundation in acting as the financial intermediary between the firm and the capital market (Figure 2.5). Financial planning is therefore concerned with the planning and management of the firm's financial needs, with regard to the alternative sources of and costs of finance. The financial needs of the firm are embodied in capital budgeting decisions on projects within the firm – "How much should we invest?" The treasury aspect of the activity is concerned with how the funds required should be raised. The flows are from the capital market, into the firm and into the project. The project in turn, generates funds, which are used to pay interest on the borrowings as well as repayment. Any surplus can then be used either as profit/dividend payments or reinvested.

Finance is also concerned with identifying the ongoing needs of the firm for funds resulting from its trading activities. Growth can often result in an unpredicted shortage of funds, if the growth process is not planned.

The literature on finance embodies useful concepts to explain the behaviour of capital markets, projects and the firm. The focus is on the monetary resources, their sources and applications as well as their costs. The management of this resource is increasingly becoming a specialist role for a treasurer, but treasurers are dependent on management for information on their actions, if they are to predict the financial consequences.

The role of the treasurer or finance manager is, firstly, to forecast and predict the cost of capital for the firm. The cost of capital will be dependent on ruling interest rates, expected yields the firm is producing, and the risk rating which has been given to the firm. Clearly, the choices in raising finance are dependent on the type of organization and the market-place. In the case of the public sector, standardized rates are usually laid down by central government. However, increasingly, even public sector organizations will be allowed to obtain funds from the market-place, alongside the private sector, in which case the cost of debt finance will be an important issue for them, just as much as for the private sector. Cost of debt finance is primarily dependent on the risk return trade off in the market-place, and the market's expectations. Alternatively, equity finance, e.g. shares, represents a further source of finance in which future expectations of earnings and the overall industrial expectations of performance will provide an indication of the cost of equity finance.

The finance manager is concerned with major investments and financing of decisions, whether these be associated with new plant and equipment, acquisitions and mergers. They must match the investment project to the capital market. Investment appraisal and capital budgeting are a significant aspect of modelling and financial planning.

The need for financial control is explicit in major projects, both of the capital costs and the working capital. The ongoing financial performance of such projects may decline through the lack of individual financial control and post-completion audits. The ongoing individual projects may get lost in the overall financial performance. It is important that day-to-day finances are managed, dealing with the cyclical and random pits and troughs of cash flow. It is the cash flow that requires management. The consumption of the cash and its generation will be dependent on the other functional activities within the firm. It is the treasury manager's role to ensure adequate provision of day-to-day finances if the firm is to avoid problems of cash shortages restricting ordinary business operations. The utilization of generated cash requires management by the treasurer, either by investment in future generators or in short-term placing within the capital markets. These are the activities considered in the finance literature.

The literature on finance also provides some guidance on the features of a good model and suggests that the current models tend to be:

- bottom-up, developed from the particular but aggregating to the total;
- accounting models, using the principle of sources and use of funds;
- deterministic and not probabilistic;
- solved crudely, often by trial and error, and rarely optimizing performance.

The literature suggests the need for certain improvements.

- Results from the model must be plausible or credible.
- The model should be flexible, so that it can be adapted and expanded to meet the circumstances, including revision of goals.
- The model should improve on current practice and facilitate learning by the user and developers.
- The inputs and the outputs of the model should be comprehensive.
- The model should incorporate interrelationships.
- The model should embody simplicity, user friendliness and comprehensibility of output (pro forma).
- The model should embody both top-down and bottom-up perspectives, reconciling the needs for detail with the strategic perspective.
- The model should recognize uncertainty and provide insight into sensitivity.
- The modeller must recognize the fallibility of the model and in particular appreciate the limitation placed on the output by the quality of input.
- The model cannot make decisions – it can only provide insight to assist decision making.

MANAGEMENT ACCOUNTING

The Accountant can assist the financial predictions by keeping records of actions taken, as well as budgeting for them. To do this, the accountant prepares balance sheets, profit and loss accounts and funds flow statements, which represent both static and dynamic models of the firm. In these models conflicting measures have been reconciled in a common monetary unit of measurement. These pro-forma statements provide a consistent window through which to view the financial progress of the firm and have been adapted by financial planners as their reporting format.

The accounting model is based on historical data collected procedurally and uses a deterministic logic. It provides comparative and analytical information through trends and ratios. However, the accounting model can be misleading, as the logic is not made explicit and pseudo-accuracy is achieved by following conventions and accounting policies consistent with validation through auditing. Economic and accounting definitions may conflict or be inconsistent. Financial analysts are very aware of the ability of these financial statements to be "window dressed", and of the short-term performance to be adjusted by creative accounting. By focusing on the long-term trends and the flow of funds, it is possible to establish a clearer picture of the performance of the firm.

Accounting information systems provide vital historic reports on financial flows, costs and the behaviour of the firm. It is therefore simple to use the accounting information as valuable empirical evidence from which to build our financial model. However, great care must be taken – where comparison is done over time, it must be of like with like. The problem is not only the firm changing over time as new equipment, new methods and new procedures are adopted, as well as new staffing policies operated, but the implications of acquisitions and mergers distort the picture. In addition, accounting systems suffer from the inherent problem of measurement with the monetary unit. As readers will know, the impact of inflation can be significant in terms of distorting the accounting reporting model. It is therefore important that, in comparison, these methods are carefully judged. Besides, the accounting systems may contain other measures, such as the operational characteristic, including hours used, rates of pay, cost per unit, sales volumes, etc. and these may be used as elements within our financial models. This is the method by which financial models such as budgets and standard cost are prepared.

As analysts external to the firm, as in the case of shareholder, creditor or even predator, we do not have access to the primary data sources. We are then dependent on our evaluation and analysis of the secondary data source as published in the annual accounts and reports. Looking through this secondary data, we must recognize not only the implications of compliance with conventions, but also the opportunity for creativity to have been used to ensure a good public image for the firm's performance. It is therefore vital that a detailed analysis is made of all the notes to the accounts, to see whether policies have been consistent, for example, in the areas of stock valuation, depreciation, etc. In addition, the impact of inflation will yet again raise its head, as will the aspect of foreign exchange where the firm trades or operates in more than one currency. This issue can be very significant, as the case of Polly Peck plc has demonstrated, where the superficial analysis of profitability failed to distinguish profits from operations from unrealizable monetary gains resulting from foreign exchange movements. Regrettably, the case demonstrated a lack of competence on the part of many analysts who had expressed unjustified confidence in the company, which subsequently collapsed. The funds flow statement should reconcile the opening and closing balance sheets with the profit and loss account. In the UK however, the accounting standard historically did not ensure a full reconciliation, although a new standard aligns British practice with that in many of our European partners and the USA. It should be the case that the funds flow statement genuinely represents a cash flow movement between opening and closing balance sheets. It is this principle that we will follow in financial planning, not the distorted historic practices of funds flow statements in the UK.

The uses of financial analysis as an estimation process and prediction for future performance are distorted significantly by mergers and acquisitions that are very common in public quoted companies. It is therefore difficult to compare like with like. However, where a comparison is possible, the use of ratios to inform us about the performance of a firm are important and represent significant parameter estimations that may be built into our financial model of the firm. For example, models of asset utilization and stock turnover are important working measures, as are profit margins and current statements about debt to equity and tax efficiency.

It is, however, the domain of management accounting, with its principle of planning and control, that has had a more consistent history of financial planning. Budgeting has been practised by management accountants from the early days of cost accounting. Budgets represent financial models of the firm built from each activity in the firm, through to the consolidation within the master budget of the profit and loss account, balance sheet and cash flow statement. The importance of the budgeting process as a financial model should not be overlooked (see Figure 2.6). It is one of the most common models of the firm, that is regularly developed within organizations. It has been developed to support strategic planning with corporate planning and the development of the five-year plan. It has also been used in the short term for operational planning and control, particularly with production and operational scheduling in standard costing. An important element of budgeting is that of feedback, in which both the plan and the action are compared, providing the opportunity to revise future budgets in line with experience. This important learning curve should be mimicked in other financial planning activities. A major shortcoming of most budgets is the failure to examine the external position in the areas of both the supply and demand markets. It is in these areas that we must depend on both finance and economics to enrich our planning process.

Management accounting can provide us with important information on the behaviour of the firm, particularly the cost and production function. Much of the theoretical framework of management accounting has been derived from economics and applied to the operation of the firm in its environment. Improvements in management accounting practice have often resulted from the addition of techniques from economics and operational research – e.g. probabilistic budgeting, decision trees, expected values. Management accountants have been very responsive to modelling technology, and particularly spreadsheets (Kaye, 1986). Unfortunately, they have predominately applied deterministic model practices, rather than exploring the available techniques.

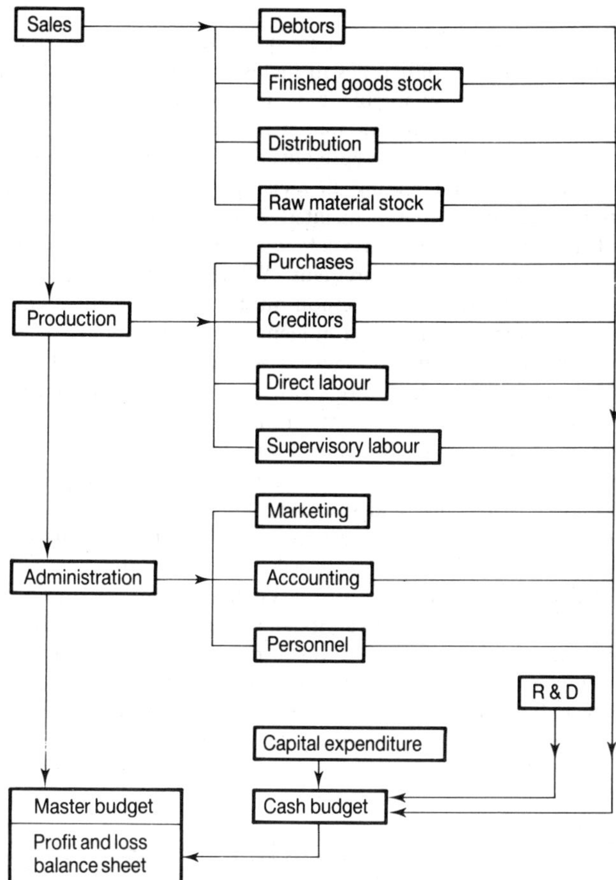

FIGURE 2.6 Diagram of budgeting model

OPERATIONAL RESEARCH

We have already made reference in the areas of finance and economics to the role of mathematics and statistics, but the embodiment of mathematical practices to solve business problems is primarily the home of operational research. Operational research is concerned with determination of the optimum course of action in a decision problem, under the restriction of limited resources (Figure 2.7). Mathematical models represent a corner-stone of operational research, but there is more to problem solving than the construction and solution of mathematical models. Mathematical models assume a quantification of the decision variables and criteria. If the criteria are qualitative rather than quantitative, then there may be difficulties in inclusion within the mathematical models. In particular, intangible benefits remain a problem for this approach (this principle equally applies to accounting). This limitation of operational research, which represents a very significant factor, should not be ignored in undertaking financial planning models. While all attempts to quantify even the qualitative data are made (using scaling and probabilities), we are always left with some elements that require justification rather than measurement. While these may be excluded from the financial model, the decision must reintroduce these elements. We must recognize that personal judgement may be applied.

Operational research may be viewed as both a science and an art. It is scientific, in that it applies mathematical techniques and algorithms to problem solving, yet it is also an art, in that it depends on creativity and the personal ability of both the analyst and decision makers. Practice of operational research includes the recognition of the appropriate technique to apply to the problem situation. This requires both experience and the knowledge of the limitations of each of the techniques. The development of the model is a crucial step in the implementation of operational research and represents a systematic stage in the decision-making process. The solution to a model, while being accurate and exact, must provide adequate representation of the decision situation. While a real situation may involve many variables and constraints, only a fraction of these variables may truly dominate the behaviour of the real system. It is the identification of the relevant elements and this simplification of

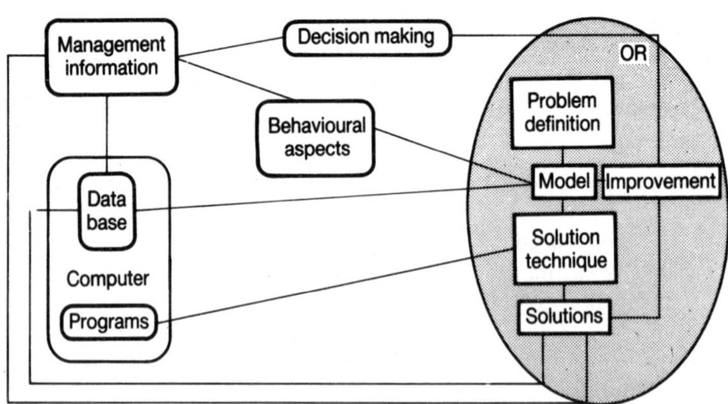

FIGURE 2.7 Territory of OR

reality that is a part of constructing models. The exclusion of an important variable from the decision model will restrict capabilities and negate its value.

The data from which the modeller has to operate, and from which the model itself will be constructed, fall into two categories. First, there are measured data, as in the case of our accounting information systems. For example, the cost of materials may be established and its usage may be a predefined measure, based on a standard. Data of this form are known as deterministic; such models are known as deterministic models. Other data are less certain and may have their origin in statistical data, which can be represented by probabilistic distribution. Such data are used in probabilistic or stochastic models.

Operational researchers have a portfolio of techniques available to solve these problems. Primarily, methods can be classified as either mathematical models or simulation. In the case of mathematical models, the objectives and constraints of the model are expressed mathematically as functions of the decision variables. In the case of simulation, there is no explicit statement of the relationships between input and output. Instead, a simulation model breaks down the model into elemental modules that are linked in well-defined logical relationships (if then). Starting from an input module, computation will move from one module to another and finally to the output result. A number of iterations will be undertaken in the case of simulation, until a steady state is established (no increases or decrease in queues), when relationships between input and output may be identified. Simulation models offer greater flexibility in representing complex systems but require a source to generate the input data. This is usually achieved by the random number generators and a computer is used to solve the extended calculation.

Solving operational research models falls into two distinct types of computation. Simulation models require repetitive computation and are time-consuming and typically are therefore restricted by the availability of computer time. Computations in mathematical models are typically iterative, in that a series of computations will be done until a constant relationship has been established which represents the optimum. This process is known as convergence towards the optimum. To succeed, tests must be carried out in the iterative process to ensure that convergence is still taking place, rather than divergence away from the optimum solution. It should be noted that the complexity of the mathematical model may make it impossible to devise a solution algorithm, in which case the model remains computationally insoluble. To overcome this, simplification must be introduced; alternatively, a non-optimum method of a solution may be introduced, such as heuristics, in which rules of thumb are introduced to obtain a good solution as opposed to the best solution.

The techniques of OR include:

- mathematical programming:
  —linear
  —integer
  —dynamic
  —goal
  —non-linear;
- deterministic, stochastic or probabilistic modelling;
- Markov chains;
- decision theory and games theory;
- network, PERT or critical path analysis;
- inventory models;
- queueing theory;
- Monte Carlo simulation.

An important element of modelling is the development of a program in which a mathematical model is structured to be solvable. It is then implemented using a mechanism for solving – i.e. programming into the computer. A mathematical model is structured by answering the following questions:

1. What does the model seek to determine (what are the unknown variables of the problem)?
2. What constraints must be imposed on the variables to satisfy the limitations of the system?
3. What is the objective or goal that needs to be achieved to determine the optimum (best) solution from amongst all the feasible values of the variables?

The phases of an operational research study are:

1. Definition of the problem.
2. Construction of the model.
3. Solution of the model.
4. Validation of the model.
5. Implementation of the final results.

SUMMARY

The four disciplines we have examined each contribute something to the common domain of financial planning. Important elements of econometrics are the external foci, reflecting the market-place in which the firm operates, and secondly, economic representation of the relationships, both within the firm and externally, in mathematical models representing the economic theory. Economics also provides techniques for handling large data sets. Finance provides us with the linkage between the financial market-place, the availability of funds and the consumption of those funds within the firm. The focus is on the financial flows between these two environments. Management accounting has an emphasis upon the (detailed) internal operation of the firm and its relationships are most clearly represented in the budget model of the firm. In addition, the accounting perspective on the firm provides a pro forma that may be used across all financial models – i.e. the balance sheet, profit and loss account and source and application of funds. Operational research provides a disciplined mathematical approach in the solving of real world problems. It identifies limitations of the mathematical models and offers solution techniques for these models. Together they allow the development of understanding assisting in the shift from diagrammatic representation of the firm to the formal notation of the model.

Collectively, these disciplines enrich our financial planning process and the models that we generate. The use of any individual one, whilst legitimate within its own discipline, may be constrained and limited by its failure to include the perspectives of the others. It is noticeable, for example, that the financial models used by bankers in leverage buy-outs have often failed to recognize the limitation of their secondary data sources. The models' estimation of parameters have lacked comparability across time, thereby failing to provide good historical data on which to build future expectations. The lack of internal understanding of the firm has led to serious misconceptions on its operation which should have been available through the management accounting data source. In addition, the financial models used have often been solved using simplification, both with the mathematical model and the computational methods. The available computer technology should not be ignored at this early stage, as our models may be restricted by our ability to solve them, given the technology we have available.

References and further reading

Brealey, R.A. and Myers, S.C. (1988) *Principles of corporate finance* (3rd edn), Maidenhead: McGraw-Hill.

Gee, K. (1986) *Advanced Management Accounting Problems,* Basingstoke: Macmillan.

Kaplan, R.S. (1982) *Advanced Management Accounting,* Hemel Hempstead: Prentice Hall.

Kaye, G.R. (1986) *The Impact of IT on Accountants,* Management Information Systems Series, Book 4, ICMA.

Koutsoyiannis, A. (1986) *Theory on Econometrics* (3rd edn), Basingstoke: Macmillan.

Lee, C.F. (1983) *Financial Analysis and Planning,* Wokingham: Addison Wesley.

Naylor, T.H., Vernon, J.M. and Wertz, K.L. (1983) *Managerial Economics,* Maidenhead: McGraw-Hill.
Porter, M.E. (1980) *Competitive Strategy,* New York: Free Press.
Scapens, R.W. (1985) *Management Accounting – A review of recent developments,* Basingstoke: Macmillan.
Schlosser, M. (1989) *Corporate Finance,* Hemel Hempstead: Prentice Hall.
Sherwood, D. (1983) *Financial Modelling Practical Guide,* London: Gee & Co.
Taha, H.A. (1987) *Operational Research,* Basingstoke: Macmillan.
Weston, J.F. and Brigham, E.F. (1987) *Essentials on Managerial Finance,* New York: Dryden Press.

3

Types of Models – Structures and Examples

INTRODUCTION

All the models that we are going to examine share a common structure and characteristics. Since our models are purposeful, we will have an output. The output will be in the form of a report of the result of our modelling process, which will provide information to assist in solving the problem. In the case of decision making, the output will provide an insight into the choice to be made from amongst the alternatives. The structure of this report is to inform decision makers and problem solvers, and on this basis the general principles of reporting and information (which are dealt with in Chapter 4) should be followed.

The use of textual, numeric, tabular and graphical output alternatives should be considered. Where alternatives are to be reviewed, then the results for individual outcomes should be generated (but the design should incorporate comparative reports).

Having selected the form of output, consideration of the available input should be given in conjunction with the logic by which the input produces the output. The logic needs to be structured, validated and documented. It will be common to the alternative outcomes but the difference will lie with the alternative assumptions embodied in the input.

The model will therefore be structured as any data processing activity, in the form shown in Figure 3.1.

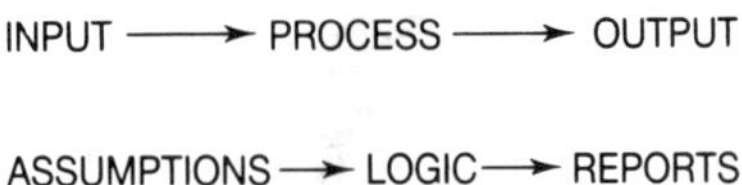

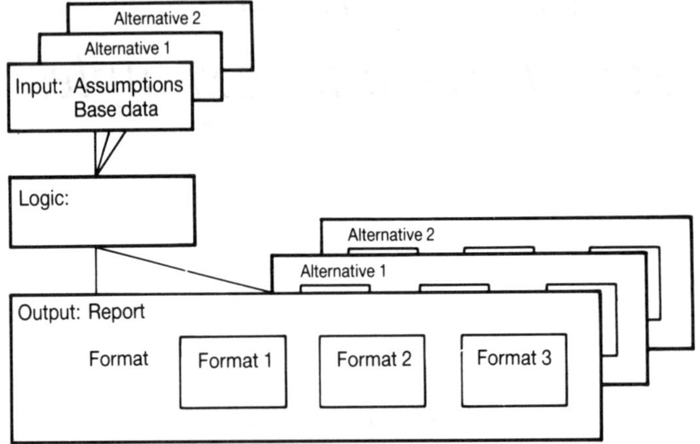

FIGURE 3.1 Structure of a model

Models may be classified according to their usage. For example, simulation models are used to simulate how a real item would behave under a given set of circumstances. The advantage of this approach is the reduction of risk and cost. An example would be a model of an aircraft, undergoing wind tunnel testing, where the model simulates the real aircraft flying, with which a major cost as well as risk would be associated (i.e. test flying an untried item). Recently Citroën announced the launch of a new car that had been designed using computer-simulation techniques to test the characteristics of the car without the need to build a prototype. This resulted in a saving of cost and time.

Optimizing models are associated with the area of operational research in which models are built using mathematical representations, such that the processing of the model will permit the calculation of an optimal solution. This approach has been substantially developed since the last war in the areas of linear programming, queueing theory, economic order quantities, etc. The advantages of this approach are that it identifies the best decision, thus eliminating the judgement normally applied by the manager. There is a problem, however, in that the mathematical representation may lead to a simplification of reality. This could eliminate essential characteristics, thus resulting in an optimal solution that may not reflect the variety existing in the environment. Thus it is still up to the individual manager to add the essential judgement basis.

Forecasting models have been available for some considerable time, based on either simple linear regression or multiple regression. The basic principle of forecasting is to project trends, cycles and seasonality into the future. This approach is effectively used in the areas of sales forecasting and budgeting decisions. It has, however, received some bad publicity resulting from the use of historic data simply projected into the future without consideration of possible future changes.

In this chapter we will provide some examples of financial models as used in the financial planning process. We will start with a simple model of cash flow forecasting, which forms an integral part of many models. We will then develop a simple simulation model to forecast profitability and the cash requirements of a company.

The percentage of sales simulation model is a good introductory model to exemplify the structure and operation of many financial models. We will subsequently develop and examine other financial models. We will examine the simultaneity of the generation of profits and the debt finance of a business, using a simple simultaneous equation-based model. This will be expanded to illustrate how a number of fundamental financial relationships may be expressed. We will then consider the financing problem and the potential opportunity for optimizing the finance mix within the firm.

The two major factors, which need further examination, are demand forecasting and the production function. For these, we will turn to econometric models and the management accounting literature, both of which provide us with insight into how we could approach the estimation and the modelling of these areas.

A FIRST MODEL – CASH FLOW FORECASTING

This first model is at the heart of many financial models. Our concern in this model is to represent the inflows and outflows of cash within the respective time periods. Cash is the essential life blood of the firm and the model must reflect the sources of cash, its application and generation within the business cycle. The simplest way to express these flows is with a diagram. The use of diagrams within the modelling process is an important tool for the expression of relationships and the flows prior to developing mathematical models. We shall return to this subject in Chapter 5, when we recommend methods of model building.

Figure 3.2 identifies the sources of cash as:

- shareholders' and proprietors' funds;
- long and short-term loans.

The applications of cash are to:

- the acquisition of fixed assets (land, buildings and machinery);
- the initiation of the working capital cycle.

The working capital cycle applies cash to purchasing materials, labour and services, converting the inputs to finished goods and sales that generate cash from receipt from debtors. The leakage from the system is of cash to pay interest on loans and service the dividends or withdrawals of profit.

Converting this diagram into a model we have maintained three key elements: The first section models the income received during a period of time. The second section models expenditure in the same time period.

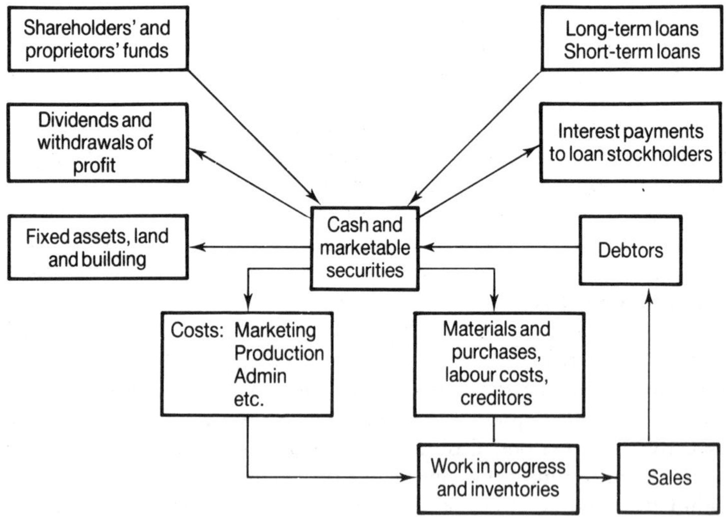

FIGURE 3.2 Cash flow cycle

The third section brings together the income and the expenditure to show a surplus or deficit in the particular period, matched to the starting cash balance at the beginning of the period and thereby generating the closing cash position.

At this stage the model would look something like this:

Cash receipts:

1. Receipts from debtors
2. Cash sales
3. Interest on deposits
4. Dividends on investments
5. Cash investments
6. Cash received for sale of fixed assets
7. Total income = Σ line 1 to 6

Cash outflow:

8. Payments for purchases
9. Wages and salaries paid
10. Expenses
11. Taxation
12. Dividends paid
13. Capital expenditure
14. Total expenditure = Σ line 8 to 13
15. **Change in cash position** = line 7 − line 14
16. **Opening cash position**$_t$ = closing cash position$_{t-1}$ (line 17)
17. **Closing cash position** = line 16 + line 15

The first problem of the model is now apparent, in that lines 16 and 17 apparently refer to each other: this expression requires further decomposition and using our previous statement, i.e. opening cash balance period t = closing cash balance in period $t-1$, we may further decompose this by stating that closing cash balance in period 0 be an input variable, then the closing cash position in period 1 is the closing cash position in period 0 plus the change in cash period 1.

This means that, for the initial period, the opening balance is defined by the input variable; thereafter it is a dependent variable. This simple model may now be built. Example 3.1 shows how this works.

In its simplest form, the cash flow forecast can be a totally deterministic model, the data for both income and expenditure being entered on the basis of assumption. Alternatively, the assumptions may in turn be modelled either within this main area or in separate models. In Example 3.1 we have incorporated elements of the creditor and debtor payment modules. This modular approach is followed in the case of budgetary

EXAMPLE 3.1

Cash flow forecast model

Workings

Sales revenue		*November*	*December*	*January*	*February*	*March*	*Qtr 1*
Sales volume		15 000	12 000	14 000	10 000	11 000	35 000
Price		1.00	1.00	1.00	1.00	1.00	
		--------	--------	--------	--------	--------	
Sales revenue		£15,000	£12,000	£14,000	£10,000	£11,000	£35,000
Debt period % in:	less month		0	0	0	0	
	one month		0	0	0	0	
	two/more		100	100	100	100	
Cash receipts				£15,000	£12,000	£14,000	£41,000

Production	*November*	*December*	*January*	*February*	*March*	*Qtr 1*
Material usage	£4 000	£4 500	£3 500	£4 500	£6 000	
Material stock change		£500	£500	£500	£500	£1 500
	-------- --	-------- --	--------	--------	--------	
Purchases	£4 000	£5 000	£4 000	£5 000	£6 500	£15 500
Credit period %	less month	0	0	0	0	
in:	one month	100	100	100	100	
	two/more	0	0	0	0	
Payments			£5 000	£4 000	£5 000	£14 000

Income	*November*	*December*	*January*	*February*	*March*	*Qtr 1*
Cash receipts			£15 000	£12 000	£14 000	£41 000
Dividends Received						£0
Interest on Deposits						£0
Capital Injections						£0
			--------	--------	--------	-------- --
Total income			£15 000	£12 000	£14 000	£41 000

Expenditure						*Qtr 1*
Purchase of materials			£5 000	£4 000	£5 000	£14 000
Wages			£1 250	£1 000	£1 250	£3 500
Overheads			£2 000	£2 000	£1 750	£5 750
Expenses			£0	£0	£0	£0
Rent and rates			£0	£0	£0	£0
Repairs and maint.			£0	£0	£0	£0
Motor expenses			£0	£0	£0	£0
Capital Expenditure			£10 000	£0	£10 000	£20 000
Dividends			£1 000	£0	£0	£1 000
			--------	--------	--------	--------
Total expenditure			£19 250	£7 000	£18 000	£44 250

Cash position	*November*	*December*	*January*	*February*	*March*	*Qtr 1*
Surplus/deficit			(£4 250)	£5 000	(£4 000)	(£3 250)
Cash B/F			£2 000	(£2 250)	£2 750	£2 000
Cash C/F		£2 000	(£2 250)	£2 750	(£1 250)	(£1 250)

models where separate elements are built of sales forecast, production, cost of sales, material purchased and manpower planning, the results from these separate models being brought together in the cash flow forecast. If this approach is followed, then no dynamic interaction exists between the sub-models. Care must therefore be taken to maintain consistency in each of the areas.

A major enhancement to the cash flow forecast could be the introduction of a constraint. A common constraint is an overdraft limit or a minimum balance status. In order to maintain the equality between the constraint and the cash balance within the model, a slack variable will be required. This is best illustrated by Example 3.2, where a constraint of an overdraft is matched by the capacity to borrow, or pay off a loan. As a result of this, interest will have to be met on any outstanding loans. Example 3.2 illustrates this situation by incorporating interest payable as an expenditure item. In this example, interest has been lagged, the interest paid in the current period being based on the loan at the end of the previous period. The repayment of the loans takes place at the end of the month only. The same approach to leads and lags has been developed in the areas of debtors and creditors in Example 3.1, where the receipts from debtors for credit sales were lagged by two months. Use of leads and lags within financial models is a common occurrence. However, in this latter case, use of a lag for interest payments is perhaps unusual. An improvement would have been to base interest on the loan for the current period, but since the loan for the current period is dependent on the shortfall between income and expenditure, we have established our first interdependency, which is represented by simultaneous equations.

PERCENTAGE OF SALES

Our next simulation model is based on modelling costs and assets as a percentage of sales and it illustrates the use of a pro forma profit and loss account, balance sheet and sources and applications of funds statement. This pro forma can be found in use in many financial plans and models. It represents the accountant's model of the firm and has been utilized both by econometricians and by finance and accounting personnel, to illustrate the status of a business. It is particularly appropriate to use this approach, as the financial performance of a firm is closely linked to the critical rate of return on capital employed. It also represents the standard reporting model used by accountants to demonstrate the status of a firm, so permits the integration of the history with the forecast. It should be noted that the three elements (profit and loss account, balance sheet and sources and applications of funds) each contributes a different modelling capability. First, the profit and loss account provides an economic

EXAMPLE 3.2

Cash flow forecast with interest payments*

B	*C*	*D*	*E*	*F*	*G*	*H*
	Actual			*Budget*		
	Prev Yr	*Year tot.*	*Qtr 1*	*Qtr 2*	*Qtr 3*	*Qtr 4*
Cash flow statement-						
Balance b/f	32 700	10 000	10 000	15 395	15 012	27 279
Sales receipts	646 273	769 331	135 739	199 926	233 277	200 389
	-----	-----	-----	-----	-----	-----
Expenditure						
Materials	173 190	209 155	30 991	58 492	59 714	59 958
Other costs & exp	82 300	77 882	10 042	22 677	23 006	22 156
Payroll	310 680	389 200	96 176	97 468	98 425	97 131
Sales tax	54 273	62 958	10 071	16 610	21 415	14 862
Income tax	20 000	5 000	5 000			
Capital exp.	25 000	25 000				25 000

	665 443	769 195	152 281	195 247	202 560	219 107
Cash for period	(19 170)	135	(16 542)	4 679	30 717	(18 719)
Interest payable	3 530	1 750	563	563	450	175
Cash before financing	10 000	8 385	(7 105)	19 512	45 279	8 385
Minimum desired	15 000	15 000	15 000	15 000	15 000	15 000
Borrowings	22 500	29 500	22 500	0	0	7 000
Repayments	22 500	22 500	0	4 500	18 000	0
Balance c/f	10 000	15 385	15 395	15 012	27 279	15 385

*This model is explored further in Chapter 5 (NB Some rounding is present in these values).

projection on a dynamic basis, usually linking sales to the profit performance. The balance sheet provides a static relationship between the assets and liabilities of the firm at a specific point in time and is represented by the fundamental economic equilibrium between assets and liabilities. The sources and application of funds statement provides a reconciliation between the opening and the closing balance sheet by explaining not only the internally generated funds resulting from the operating performance as represented in the profit and loss account, but in addition the management of the assets and liabilities. The sources and application of funds statement is the cash flow forecast, and in many countries the terms "funds flow" or "cash flow forecasts" are used in place of "sources and application of funds".

An extension of the cash flow forecast would be to incorporate the profit and loss account relationships within the dynamics of the business. This could be matched to the closing state of the business in a closing balance sheet. This then is a simple pro forma layout that we shall adopt in subsequent models.

Perhaps, the simplest model to demonstrate the relationship is the percentage of sales model. In this model, sales are used as the driver, not only for the costs that are incurred and thereby the profits generated, but also to represent the assets required to generate the sales volume and therefore finances required to maintain the balance in the balance sheet.

A key issue in finance is the linking of future requirements for funds with the application of the funds. Influences on the firm's future well-being include:

- demand for its products;
- changes in the market structure;
- changes in the supply position;
- changes in technology;
- changes in the political and social scene.

Demand is the most significant of these influences, and our first model utilizes sales as the driver for forecasting future financing needs. To simplify, we shall take demand as given (i.e. an input variable).

In this model we shall express the financial structure of the firm as a percentage of the sales. This will allow the model to dynamically reflect the changes in sales in the financial structure. As a result, the change in sales will define the change in finance.

The initial position is shown in Example 3.3.

EXAMPLE 3.3

Base position

		Base
Sales	100.00%	400
Cost of sales	90.00%	360
	--------------	----------
Profit	10.00%	40
Dividend	6.00%	24
	--------------	----------
Retained	4.00%	16
	--------------	----------
Fixed assets	75.00%	300
Current assets:		
stock	50.00%	200
debtors	22.50%	90
cash	2.50%	10
Current liabilities:		
loan short-term	2.50%	10
creditors	10.00%	40
accruals	12.50%	50
	--------------	----------
Working capital	50.00%	200
Capital employed	125.00%	500
	--------------	----------
Financed by:		
shares	12.50%	50
retained earnings	75.00%	300
	--------------	----------
Equity	87.50%	350
Debentures	37.50%	150
--------------	----------	
Total	125.00%	500
	======	=====

Our assumptions are that:

- the capital employed is dependent on the level of sales activity and as a result the level of finance is dependent on sales. This means that given an exiting equilibrium any change in sales volume will result in a change in the level of finance;
- the plant is already at full capacity and any change in sales will immediately have to be met by an increase in capacity necessitating the increase in fixed assets;
- all costs and relationships are linear.

These assumptions have implications on the validity of the model to reality which are reflected in:

- the simplification of the model;
- its predictive capacity;
- its sensitivity to changes.

In addition, the dynamic capacity of the model is restricted by these assumptions:

- a single driving force: sales;
- all other variables constant or dependent.

If we now add an additional forecast column for sales in the next year, we can utilize the relationships of sales to the financial structure to forecast the subsequent finance requirements.

EXAMPLE 3.4

Forecast state

		Base	*Forecasts*
Sales	100.00%	400	500
Cost of sales	90.00%	360	450
	--------------	----------	----------
Profit	10.00%	40	50
Dividend	6.00%	24	30
	---------------	----------	----------
Retained	4.00%	16	20
	---------------	----------	----------
Fixed assets	75.00%	300	375
Current assets:			
stock	50.00%	200	250
debtors	22.50%	90	112.5
cash	2.50%	10	12.5

Current liabilities:			
loan short-term	2.50%	10	10
creditors	10.00%	40	50
accruals	12.50%	50	62.5
	--------------	----------	----------
Working capital	50.00%	200	252.5
Capital employed	125.00%	500	627.5
	--------------	----------	----------
Financed by:			
shares	12.50%	50	50
retained earnings	75.00%	300	320
	--------------	----------	----------
Equity	87.50%	350	370
Debentures	37.50%	150	150
	--------------	----------	----------
Total	125.00%	500	520
	========	=========	=========
Additional finance required:			107.5

The possible ways of raising the additional finance include:

- reducing the dividend;
- increasing the equity stock;
- borrowing short-term debt;
- borrowing long-term debt;
- reducing the investment in working capital;
- reducing the investment in fixed assets.

All these options can now be explored after we have a forecast. However, it is likely that there will be conditions attached to any finance and differences in the costs of capital. To improve the model's capabilities, we may set financing mix criteria, thereby enabling the model to indicate the sources of finance that will enable the equality of the balance sheet to be maintained.

EXAMPLE 3.5

Additional finance required

Maximum debt	50% of total assets	375
Max current liabilities	1/3 of current assets	125

Mix of finance:	Short-term loans	2.5
	Long-term loans	100
	Equity	5

	Total	107.5

This results in a forecast as follows:

Revised forecast

	%	*Base*	*Forecasts*
Sales	100.00%	400	500
Cost of sales	90.00%	360	450
	---------------	----------	----------
Profit	10.00%	40	50
Dividend	6.00%	24	30
	---------------	----------	----------
Retained	4.00%	16	20
	---------------	----------	----------
Fixed assets	75.00%	300	375
Current assets:			
stock	50.00%	200	250
debtors	22.50%	90	112.5
cash	2.50%	10	12.5
Current liabilities:			
loan short-term	2.50%	10	12.5
creditors	10.00%	40	50
accruals	12.50%	50	62.5
	---------------	----------	----------
Working capital	50.00%	200	250
Capital employed	125.00%	500	625
	---------------	----------	----------
Financed by:			
shares	12.50%	50	55
retained earnings	75.00%	300	320
	---------------	----------	----------
Equity	87.50%	350	375
Debentures	37.50%	150	250
	---------------	----------	----------
Total	125.00%	500	625
	=========	=========	=========

The logic of this model is as follows:

Sales	input
Cost of sales =	90% × sales
Profit =	sales − cost of sales
Dividend =	6% × sales
Retained =	Profit − dividend
Fixed assets =	75% × sales
Current assets:	
stock =	50% × sales
debtors =	22.5% × sales
cash =	2.5% × sales
Current liabilities:	
loan short-term =	constant
creditors =	10% × sales
accruals =	12.5% × sales
Working capital =	current assets − current liabilities
Capital employed =	fixed assets + working capital
Financed by:	
Shares:	constant
Retained earnings:	balance brought forward + retained
Equity:	shares + retained balance
Debentures:	constant
Total:	equity + debt

The limitations of the percentage of sales model are as follows.

1. Costs are assumed to be linear. This assumption is only valid over a very restricted range, as it is reasonable to assume that economies and diseconomies of scale exist. In addition, the concept of the learning curve may have an application.
2. The linear relationship between sales and fixed assets and investment in working capital is doubtful. However, the capital intensity ratio (i.e. the utilization of fixed assets) combined with the assumption of full capacity implies a requirement for increased investment in order to meet increased sales. It is likely that fixed assets are lumpy, reflecting a stepped function. This stepped structure would also apply to shift-work, which would be an alternative method of coping with increased demand.
3. The assumption of linearity may be more justified in the working capital, where sales to receipts from debtors are likely to be lagged. Similarly, creditors may be linear to production activity but in both cases the lags may be due to custom and the prevailing economic

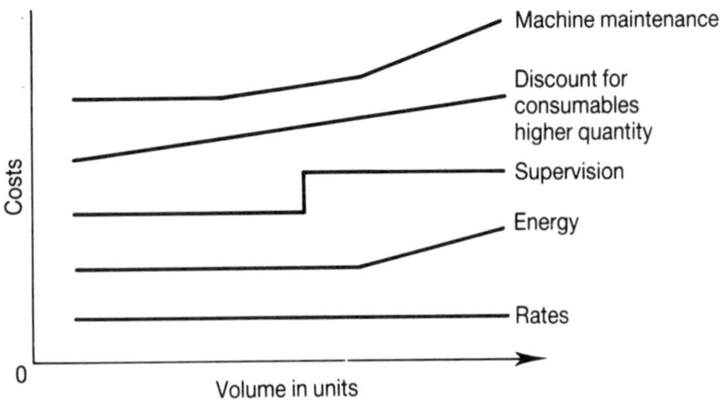

FIGURE 3.3 Graph of non-linear costs

climate. Stock levels are a buffer between production capacity and demand, but significantly are likely to increase with a fall in demand, rather than decreasing in line with sales (the use of reductions in drivers such as sales often rigorously test models and assist in identifying major weaknesses in assumptions).

4. Perhaps the major shortcoming of the model is its assumption of sales as the sole driver. An improvement would be the recognition of the demand function and the influences of both the market and the firm on the level of demand. In addition, there are likely to be seasonal as well as economic trends and cycles.
5. The model does not incorporate a cost of debt finance (i.e. interest), nor does it reflect the relative costs of alternative finance.
6. The model initially produces a forecast of financial resources but does not attempt to optimize the mix of finance to maximize the return on capital employed.
7. The model avoids the problem of equilibrium of the balance sheet by incorporating both constants and balancing values. It is only possible to solve the financial mix by a further set of equations in the sub-model.
8. The detailed relationships between variables have been ignored within the overall simplified framework. The complex relationship between sales, debtors and income has been incorporated as a linear relationship but incorporates both lags and distributions of behaviour. More detailed understanding may stem from ratio analysis.

While the percentage of sales approach has major limitations, it does illustrate the structure of a financial model and how it may be used dynamically to identify the finances required to run the firm. It should not be rejected altogether, but should be viewed as a first version from which can be evolved further models to match the characteristics of the firm and the problem specification.

ALTERNATIVE MODELS

A number of models have been developed from the basic percentage of sales model to overcome some of the limitations we have identified. The following models each offer improvement in one or more domain. The first major improvement was the inclusion of optimization of the finance mix (Carleton, 1970) and performance of the investments. The next step was the incorporation of external factors through the two areas of market-place and finance mix. The latter was first developed in the model by Warren and Shelton (1971), who developed a simple simultaneity structure. This was further developed by Francis and Rowell (1978) to incorporate the market share factors. Both these models have formed a substantial basis for many of the subsequent finance models in use.

Carleton's model

Carleton (1970) developed a model to optimize the finance mix using a linear programming approach. His model recognized the interrelationship that existed between capital budgeting, new borrowings and debt repayment, stock (share) issues and repurchase, and dividends and interest on debt (Figure 3.4).

The objective function describes the firm as seeking to maximize with respect to the time vectors of its financial decision variables, reflected in a discounted stream of future dividends and terminal share price.

Warren and Shelton's model

Warren and Shelton (1971) developed a model which not only incorporated elements of the market-place, but which also recognized the simultaneity of key relationships such as debt to interest and profit retention (Figure 3.5).

They segmented their model into four areas covering:

- sales and operating income projections;
- assets required to support sales activity level;
- funds required to provide assets;
- implications for earnings per share, market prices of shares and return on capital employed.

They expressed these relationships in the form of twenty semi-simultaneous equations, shown in Figure 3.6.

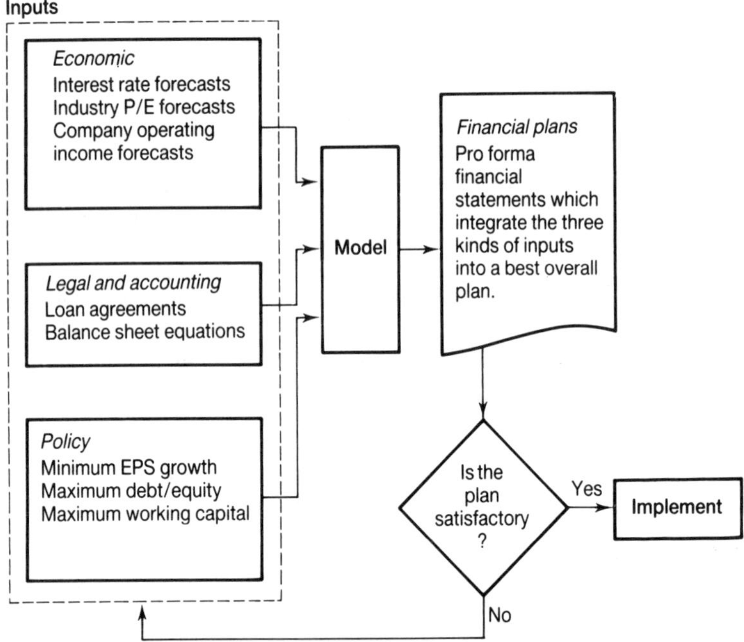

FIGURE 3.4 Carleton's model

Francis and Rowell

Francis and Rowell (1978) developed the approach adopted by Warren and Shelton, but incorporated the external environment for demand and the financial risks. Their model permitted exploration of alternative "what if?" scenarios, providing sensitivity of the model and the assumptions (Figure 3.7).

Simultaneity

A key feature of both the Warren and Shelton and the Francis and Rowell models was the use of simultaneous equations. The solving of simultaneous equations is problematic. Normally the problem is resolved in a number of ways:

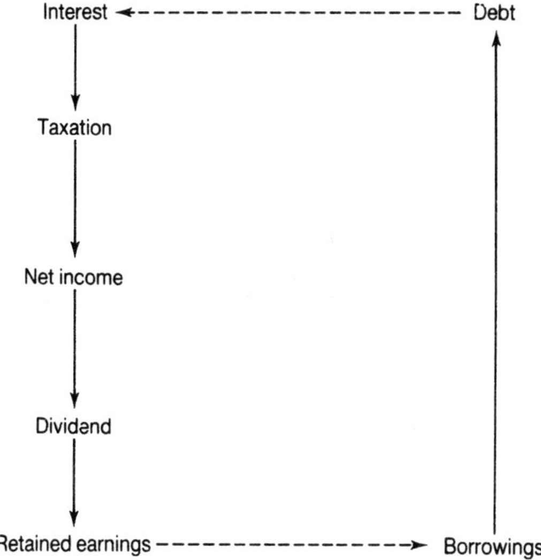

FIGURE 3.5 Warren and Shelton's Model

- ignore it: either use an approximation or substitute a lag;
- solve the equation algebraically in the model;
- incorporate an iterative process to allow the model to find a solution.

Ignoring the problem and substituting another approach is popular, but necessitates restructuring of the model and may result in a significant error in the forecast. The second method is not advisable: if the logic is extended or changed subsequently, the simultaneous equations will have to be reworked and new algebraic expressions incorporated. The third method is therefore the most widely used, and has been known as the Gauss-Sedel method of programming into the computer. By iteration around the equations and testing for equality, it is possible for the model to progress to the solution. The iterative process available in spreadsheets is particularly crude (manual definition of iterations) and caution should be observed in their usage. Improvements may be achieved by use of macros which test equality to control the iterations. Recently, the incorporation of goal-seeking capabilities has enabled spreadsheets to "solve" equations as modelling systems (Example 3.6, p. 56).

I. *Generation of sales and earnings before interest and taxes for period* t.

(1) $\text{SALES}_t = \text{SALES}_t (1 + \text{GSALS}_t)$

(2) $\text{EBIT}_t = \text{REBIT}_t \, \text{SALES}_t - \text{CEBIT}_t$

II. *Generation of total assets required for period* t.

(3) $\text{CA}_t = \text{RCA}_t \, \text{SALES}_t + \text{CCA}_t$

(4) $\text{FA}_t = \text{RFA}_t \, \text{SALES}_t + \text{CFA}_t$

(5) $A_t = \text{CA}_t + \text{FA}_t + \text{OA}_t$

III. *Financing the desired level of assets.*

(6) $\text{CL}_t = \text{RCL}_t \, \text{SALES}_t + \text{CCL}_t$

(7) $\text{NF}_t = (\text{A}_t - \text{CL}_t - \text{PFDSK}_t) - (L_{t-1} - \text{LR}_t) - S_{t-1} - R_{t-1} - b_t \{(1 - T_t) [\text{EBIT}_t - i_{t-1} (L_{t-1} - \text{LR}_t)] - \text{PFDIV}_t\}$

(8) $\text{NF}_t + B_t (1 - T_t) [i^e_t \, \text{NL}_t + U^l_t \text{NL}_t] = \text{NL}_t + \text{NS}_t$

(9) $L_t = L_{t-1} - \text{LR}_t + \text{NL}_t$

(10) $S_t = S_{t-1} + \text{NS}_t$

(11) $R_t = R_{t-1} + b_t \{(1 - T_t) [\text{EBIT}_t - i_t L_t - U^l_t \text{NL}_t] - \text{PFDIV}_t\}$

(12) $$i_t = i_{t-1} \left(\frac{L_{t-1} - \text{LR}_t}{L_t} \right) + i^e_t \frac{\text{NL}_t}{L_t}$$

(13) $$\frac{L_t}{S_t + R_t} = K_t$$

IV. *Generation of per share data for period* t.

(14) $\text{EAFCD}_t = (1 - T_t) [\text{EBIT}_t - i_t L_t - U^l_t \text{NL}_t] - \text{PFDIV}_t$

(15) $\text{CMDIV}_t = (1 - b_t) \, \text{EAFCD}_t$

(16) $\text{NUMCS}_t = \text{NUMCS}_{t-1} + \text{NEWCS}_t$

(17) $$\text{NEWCS}_t = \frac{\text{NS}_t}{(1 - U^s_t) \, P_t}$$

(18) $P_t = m_t \text{EPS}_t$

(19) $$\text{EPS}_t = \frac{\text{EAFCD}_t}{\text{NUMCS}_t}$$

(20) $$\star\text{DPS}_t = \frac{\text{CMDIV}_t}{\text{NUMCS}_t}$$

FIGURE 3.6 Equations for the Warren and Shelton model

List of unknowns and list of parameters provided by management

Unknowns	
1. SALES_t	Sales
2. CA_t	Current Assets
3. FA_t	Fixed Assets
4. A_t	Total Assets
5. CL_t	Current Payables
6. NF_t	Needed Funds
7. EBIT_t	Earnings Before Interest and Taxes
8. NL_t	New Debt
9. NS_t	New Stock
10. L_t	Total Debt
11. S_t	Common Stock
12. R_t	Retained Earnings
13. i_t	Interest Rate on Debt
14. EAFCD_t	Earnings Available for Common Dividends
15. CMDIV_t	Common Dividends
16. NUMCS_t	Number of Common Shares Outstanding
17. NEWCS_t	New Common Shares Issued
18. P_t	Price Per Share
19. EPS_t	Earnings Per Share
20. DPS_t	Dividends Per Share
Provided by Management	
21. SALES_{t-1}	Sales in Previous Period
22. GSALS_t	Growth in Sales
23. RCA_t	Current Assets as a Percent of Sales
24. RFA_t	Fixed Assets as a Percent of Sales
25. RCL_t	Current Payables as a Percent of Sales
26. PFDSK_t	Preferred Stock
27. PFDIV_t	Preferred Dividends
28. L_{t-1}	Debt in Previous Period
29. LR_t	Debt Repayment
30. S_{t-1}	Common Stock in Previous Period
31. R_{t-1}	Retained Earnings in Previous Period
32. b_t	Retention Rate
33. T_t	Average Tax Rate
34. i_{t-1}	Average Interest Rate in Previous Period
35. i_t	Expected Interest Rate on New Debt
36. REBIL_t	Operating Income as a Percent of Sales

FIGURE 3.6 Contd.

37. U^{1}_{t}	Underwriting Cost of Debt
38. U^{E}_{t}	Underwriting Cost of Equity
39. K_t	Ratio of Debt to Equity
40. $NUMCS_{t-1}$	Number of Common Shares Outstanding in Previous Period
41. m_t	Price-Earnings Ratio
42. OA_t	Other Assets
43 }	Stock/Current Assets
44 }	Debtors/Current Assets
45 }	Cash/Current Assets
46. CCA_t	Current Assets Constant
47. CFA_t	Fixed Assets Constant
48. CCL_t	Current Payables Constant
49. $CEBIT_t$	Operating Income Constant

From Warren, J.M. and J.P. Shelton, "A simultaneous-equation approach to financial planning", *Journal of Finance* (December 1971): Table 1. Reprinted by permission.

FIGURE 3.6 Contd.

EXAMPLE 3.6

Iteration

Iteration	*Opening balance*	*Opening + interest*	*Interest on overdraft*	*Closing balance*
0	100	120	0	not calculated
1	100	120	11	131
2	100	131	11.55	131.55
3	100	131.55	11.5775	131.5775
4	100	131.5775	11.578875	131.578875
5	100	131.578875	11.578943	131.578943
6	100	131.578943	11.578947	131.578947
7	100	131.578947	11.578947	131.578947
8	100	131.578947	11.578947	131.578947

At the beginning of the loop, overdraft = final overdraft

and interest $= \dfrac{(\text{overdraft} + \text{overdraft}_{t-1})}{2} \times \text{rate}$

final overdraft = trial overdraft + interest

at the end of the iteration: overdraft = final overdraft

Demand forecasting

A fault in these finance-based models has been the over-emphasis on the finance function, rather than the operational characteristics of the market-place and the production operation. In order to develop these areas we must turn away from the finance literature to econometrics. The first model we would wish to look at is demand forecasting.

Two approaches may be followed concerning demand forecasting and its incorporation into financial models. First, analysis may be undertaken to determine the shape of the demand function, which in turn is used to build a sales forecasting model. The sales forecasting model then becomes the driver for a model, such as the percentage of sales. An alternative is to incorporate the estimation of demand into the financial model, through the use of a regression function in the model. Using this approach, data is fed into the model as the first stage of building the forecast.

Demand forecasting requires an external focus on the market, the competition, the operations, the market-place. A simple demand function may be described as being:

$$S = f(D, C, E, S_{t-n}, e)$$

where: S is the sales in the forecast period;
D is the managerial decision variable, reflecting policy and spending on advertising, quality and technical innovation;
C is the competitive variable;
E is the external variable;
S_{t-n} is the lagged effect of prior sales performance;
e is the random error in the system.

While the above may only be a generalized model, a number of generic models are in use, reflecting varying degrees of simplicity. In practice not only will the respective parameters of these variables require estimation, but also the structure of the market and its behaviour will necessitate significant restructuring of the model. However, a few examples are worth demonstrating:

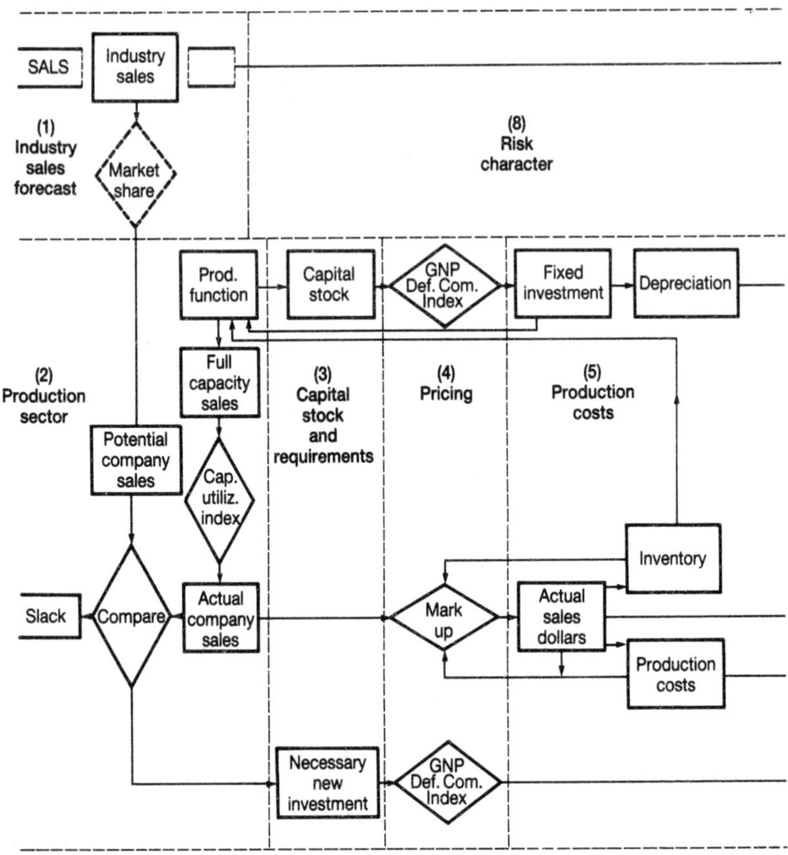

FIGURE 3.7 Francis and Rowell's model

Linear demand function

$$S = a + b \text{ Price} + c \text{ Advertising} + d \text{ Rivalry} + f \text{ GNP} + e$$

where price, advertising, rivalry in the market and the gross national product (GNP) are the variables and a is constant and e the random error, while b, c, d, f are the parameters of the variables.

More frequently, we find that demand is not linear, reflecting the changing elasticity of demand. This demand function may be modelled as:

$$S = a \times \text{Price}^b \times \text{Advertising}^c \times \text{Rivalry}^d \times \text{GNP}^f$$

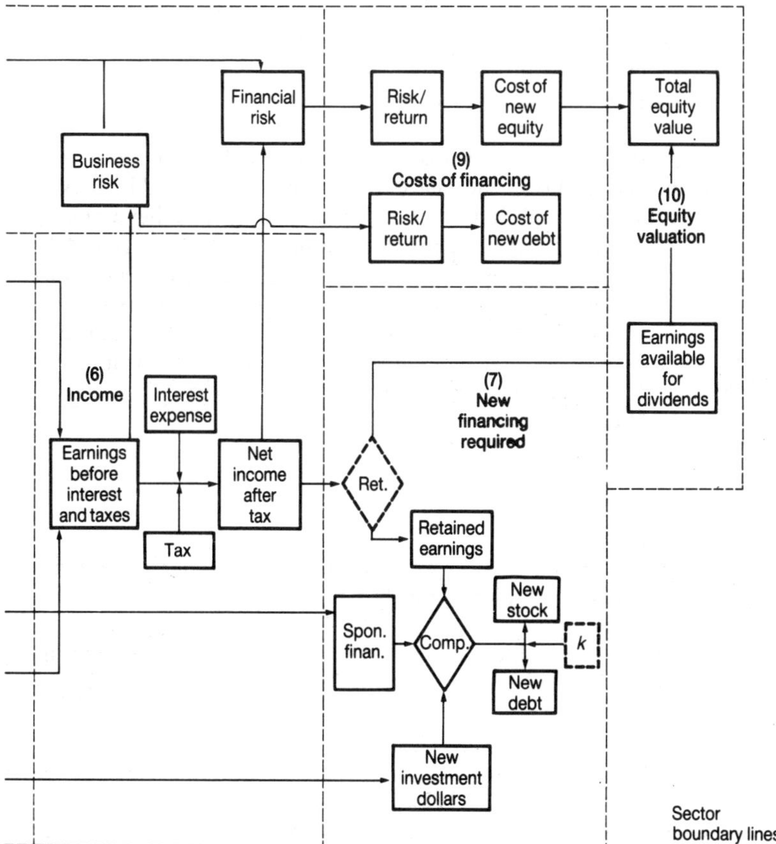

FIGURE 3.7 Contd.

Exponential demand functions such as the above may be solved by using log scales to equate back to linear models that may be solved with linear regression. Differentiation demonstrates the retention of interdependency of the variables and the effect of marginal changes in any single variable on the overall demand. In addition, the elasticity can be demonstrated again to be reflected in the values of the parameters a, b, c, d, f.

The major problem with demand forecasting is obtaining appropriate data to enable the modelling to be undertaken. Individual firms may suffer from incomplete knowledge of the market, rivalry and buyer behaviour. The use of market research methods will facilitate some improvement, as will the role of trade associations in enabling sharing of data without disabling fair competition. In all cases, the results will be a mass of data requiring analysis to facilitate the establishment of a structure and to define the behaviour of the variables. The use of statistical methods will illuminate the data and enable not only the identification of the variables and estimation of the parameters but also provide insight into the quality of the data and the estimates. It should be stressed, however, that the identification of the variables requires either a preconception or tentative theory of the likely structure of the demand function, or the ability to recognize patterns from the data. Experience of the market and its behaviour will greatly assist this process, as will expertise in statistical techniques. There are a number of organizations such as market research consultancies which provide these services to companies that cannot justify the full-time employment of such experts.

The standard techniques employed include:

- ordinary least squares;
- T-test of standard errors;
- linear regression;
- R-square measure of strength of association (1 = perfect match of estimate and actual plot, 0 totally random);
- multiple regression;
- F-statistic, which indicates whether the R-square is reliable and therefore the explanatory power of the variables in the multiple regression.

The ability to process data statistically is greatly assisted by the use of a suitable statistical package such as SPSS or Minitab, but in their absence many spreadsheet packages incorporate the essential facilities for undertaking statistical analysis. However, care must be exercised with spreadsheets, whose user-friendliness regrettably fails to ensure good practice on the part of the user. In all cases an adequate number of observations must be available (at least ten).

There are some significant problems that may be encountered in parameter estimation:

- multicollinearity, where interdependence between the right-hand independent variables restricts the ability to identify their individual contribution towards the dependent variable;
- auto-correlation may be encountered in time series where the assumption is that the error is random. Instead of being uncorrelated, values in different time periods are correlated;
- simultaneity, where interdependence exists as in simultaneous equations;

- bias – the ordinary least squares method will develop a bias where simultaneity exists but may be overcome by the use of a two-stage process;
- identification – bias in the data sample and in the perception of the modeller leading to inclusion and exclusion of variables is difficult to measure but can be significant.

Frequently the forecaster will be presented with a time series from which he has to develop his model. Two approaches may be taken here: first, they may choose to take the time series and apply it immediately to the model by incorporation of a regression function in the model; or they may attempt to analyse the model and identify the underlying factors. If the latter approach is pursued then not only the trend line must be identified, but also the seasonality and cyclical factors. A substantial number of observations will be required to enable analysis to take place, amplifying the dangers of significant structural changes in the market resulting from mergers, new entrants, and innovations.

The whole discipline of marketing has developed on the basis of understanding consumer behaviour and the market-place. Sometimes the markets are relatively easy to model, in that they are bounded and the products are clearly differentiated with segmentation, such that seepage between one market and another does not distort events. However, the modelling of consumer behaviour and of markets has its own literature and we will not attempt to cover it here.

PRODUCTION FUNCTION

We have already indicated that there is a need to incorporate the internal dynamics of the firm. These are primarily represented by the production function, which seeks to explain the relationships between inputs and outputs. To the economist, this is contained in the statement $Q = f(L,K)$ where Q is the output and L and K represent inputs. The objective is to maximize output with respect to the input, and where a degree of substitution is possible by one input for another, then we seek to minimize the cost input.

The cost accountant or management accountant has developed the work of the economist to explore the cost behaviour of individual organizations. In doing so, he has not only employed the economist's models but in addition has sought detailed production knowledge from the engineer to assist development of cost behaviour models. While the cost literature is dominated by the monetary measurement of resources and their utilization, the underlying physical behaviour must not be ignored as it will provide detailed information on substitutability and mixes as well as constraints. The cost accountant seeks to identify fixed and variable costs to enable simple forecasting models to be developed. In addition he may well develop detailed cost analysis of products and processes reflected in standard costing and budgetary models. Neither of these modelling areas should be ignored in this study, but we will encourage the reader to turn to the cost accounting and management accounting literature for detailed coverage. We would stress at this stage that the modeller with access to detailed internal cost information should be able to exploit this information in all models of the firm. This is a significant advantage not available to the external modeller and can be reflected in a powerful defence model in contested take-overs.

The simple fixed and variable linear costs of the break-even chart should not mislead the reader into over-simplification (Figure 5.5). An alternative to this picture is of course a contribution graph, which could be produced with multi-product elements – see Figure 3.8. But again this graph may well have been built up from a major simplification of the cost elements.

The cost elements may be described as being fixed costs or variable costs. First, a fixed cost is a cost which in a given period (normally the year) is not expected to change and it remains fixed in relation to the volume of throughput. This picture is only accurate, however, if we recognize it in a context of a narrow band of feasibility.

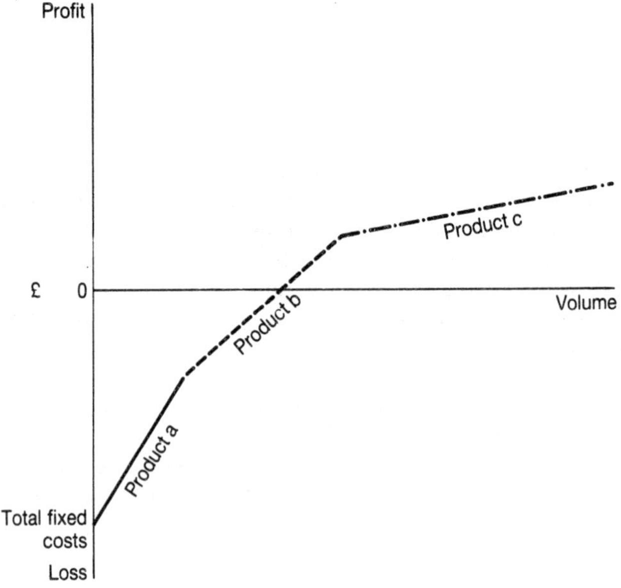

FIGURE 3.8 Contribution graph of multiple products

An example of a fixed cost could be rates, in that our rates bill is fixed during an annual period and is unlikely to change in relation to the volume of throughput. However, rates are related to the size of the business in physical terms. Normally the rateable value will be based on the size of the building, its location and its potential rental value – if we increase our size of building in response to increased demand and increased plant capacity, then immediately our level of rates will rise, and hence a stepped function would apply to the graph. However, during any period of time we will operate in a relatively narrow band of feasibility as it is not a straightforward matter to increase the size of our building or decrease it as our volume changes.

Variable costs are said to vary with the volume. Normally we are concerned with the product and sales volume; however, the cost may vary more directly with some other intermediary variable. An example could be energy consumption varying with machine usage, which is itself dependent on production volume, although it is not directly related.

In addition to fixed costs and variable costs there is a multitude of semi-variable and semi-fixed costs, some of which are illustrated in Figure 3.3 earlier. While statistical techniques are considerably easier for linear models, it is more than likely that costs will behave in a variety of ways, such as linear, curvilinear (learning curve), stepped, discontinuous, etc. These details must not be ignored if we seek representative models.

The operational researcher has greatly assisted the accountant's work by modelling the cost–profit relationships in the area of multiple products and inputs. This has resulted in effective linear programming models being used in industries as diverse as feed compounding and petroleum refining to optimize the profitability of the manufacturing process.

The question is, how do we obtain the relationships between the cost and volume? Traditionally, academics would argue for the application of regression analysis and correlation; a simplification could be the scatter graph. However, in practice it is found to be very difficult to analyse the relationship between costs and volume, even when technical analysis is undertaken. It is, however, worth trying to undertake these activities, and since each manager is responsible for a different set of costs it is his or her responsibility to obtain that relationship and model it. In this way the cost–volume relationships are based on experience. This building up of the understanding is an essential element of management and is facilitated further by the modelling process.

As in econometrics, there are two primary ways of estimating cost and production behaviour. First, there is the engineering or hypothesis-based approach. Here an explanatory model is developed from the individual parts (bottom-up), based on work measurement and observation. It may be likened to the *a priori* approach in which theories are subject to refutation. The disadvantage of this approach is the expense and the rigidity, but the major shortfall is the failure to recognize that not all costs are observable (opportunity and intangible costs).

The second approach is the historical analysis of data, in which statistical analysis seeks to identify the underlying causal relationships and patterns of cost behaviour. The techniques used are as in demand forecasting. The major shortcomings include the lack of stability in the measurement of data due to inflation, changes in accounting policies and practices and the problems of allocations or attribution of indirect costs.

Some of the problems in both methods can be overcome by the application of techniques such as indexation, activity measurement, etc. Alternatively, the combination of both approaches can provide contrasting insights enabling further analysis.

The recent debate on activity-based costing has returned the focus of management and cost accounting to the detailed analysis of the firm and the production function from a bottom-up perspective. This approach requires the modeller to develop insightful models reflecting the complexity of behaviour that illuminates the problem area and provides important learning opportunities.

OTHER RELATIONSHIPS IN THE MODEL

Many other relationships may exist in the financial models that we are building and these may be explored in the development of the model. In this way the model becomes a learning process available to management to gain understanding of their business.

For example, we have mentioned production capacity as a limiting factor and as a key element in the development of the model. Production capacity is reflected in the plan itself and is of course treated as fixed assets in the financial models. If we need to increase production capacity then we need to increase the fixed assets, requiring additional capital investment and therefore an appropriate cash flow and a consequent change in the balance sheet structure. This is a relationship that we must incorporate in the model to reflect the dynamic structure.

Another example would be the relationship between sales volume, debtors and cash flow. Here we recognize that the sales that we generate will result in delayed receipt of the revenue that may even be discounted in order to encourage customers to pay. They will be identified in the final balance sheet as debtors, but in the interim period the amounts are incorporated in the cash flow statement as receipts as and when received. The control of the credit taken by our customers, the level of doubtful debts and bad debt write-off, is reflected in our spending on credit control and in the administration budget.

Another example would be the linking of stock levels to production capacity; hence if we have a heavily seasonal business activity, then we would have to smooth our production over the year. This might result in stock build-ups prior to peak demand. A classic example of this could be Easter egg demand from the confectioners. In recognizing this stock build-up we must consider the consequent cash flows which lead to an investment in stocks, and the cost of the stocks not only in terms of the cost of capital tied up but also in terms of warehousing charges and potential deterioration of the stock whilst housed.

While we have mentioned just three isolated cases, it is critical that the management understands these relationships that are normally expressed in the traditional hierarchy of ratios used by accountants analysing the performance of the business. Figure 3.9 incorporates the ratios in a pyramid form, illustrating some of the relationships that we are concerned with.

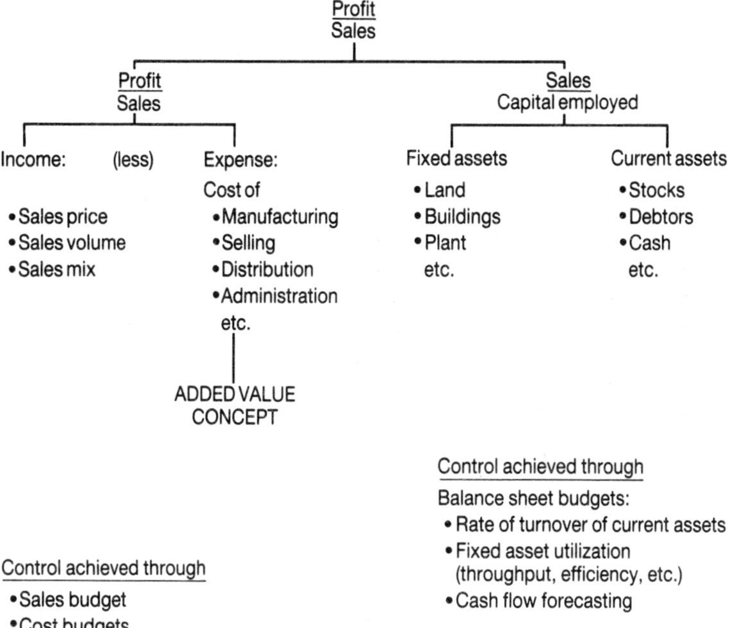

FIGURE 3.9 Dupont pyramid of financial performance ratios

SUMMARY

In this chapter we have covered the key elements of financial models:

- Financial models must reflect the financial flows represented by the movements of cash, as well as resources measured in monetary terms.
- Models require drivers such as sales or demand which provide the input variable to the forecasting model.
- Models should reflect the problem elements, and could include measures of demand, production, financial structure and performance.
- Models should produce output that is intelligible to the users. The use of pro forma style (profit and loss account, balance sheet, cash flow) enables consistent reports to be produced.
- Models should incorporate relevant detail for adequate representation.
- Modelling techniques may be exploited to overcome complexity in the system, leads, lags, simultaneity, etc.
- The quality of the model will reflect the quality of the available data and the analytical process, as well as the chosen model structure.

References and further reading

Brealey, R.A. and Myers, S.C. (1988) *Principles of Corporate Finance,* (3rd edn) Maidenhead: McGraw-Hill.

Carleton, W.T. (1970) "Analytical Model for Long Range Financial Planning", *Journal of Finance,* 25, pp. 291–315.

Francis, J.C. and Rowell, D.R. (1978) "A Simultaneous Equation Model of the Firm for Financial Analysis and Planning", *Financial Management,* Spring, pp. 29–44.

Higgins, J.C. (1980) *Strategic and Operational Planning Systems – Principles and Practice,* Hemel Hempstead: Prentice Hall.

Lee, C.F. (1983) *Financial Analysis and Planning – Theory and Applications: A Book of Readings,* Wokingham: Addison Wesley.

Naylor, T.H., Vernon, J.M. and Wertz, K.L. (1983) *Managerial Economics,* Maidenhead: McGraw-Hill.

Schlosser, M. (1989) *Corporate Finance,* Hemel Hempstead: Prentice Hall.

Warren, J. and Shelton, J. (1971) "A Simultaneous Equation Approach to Financial Planning", *Journal of Finance,* 26, pp. 1123–42.

Weston, J.F. and Brigham, E.F. (1987) *Essentials of Managerial Finance,* New York: Dryden Press.

4

Life Cycle of a Model

INTRODUCTION

The advantages and disadvantages of models were described earlier, in Chapter 1. These factors should be clearly understood before starting on the model-building process.

A model is built by a process of abstraction from reality, changing attributes and relationships into mathematical symbols. Symbolic models, though the mathematics might seem complex, are often much simpler to construct than physical models. When data are fed to the model they are manipulated according to certain rules and a result is produced. Both data and rules can be changed so that the model reflects the real world. It is a process of converting implicit accounting activities into explicit algorithms. The process may be tackled in stages by developing simple models and subsequently amplifying them into more complex, detailed models. In Chapter 1 we described the evolution of a new model from an existing one, as applied to budgeting, but this principle is generalizable to all modelling situations. This process of evolution embodies our conceptualization of the real world problem and our learning about it through the modelling process. Figure 1.1 illustrated this conceptualization process as a series of iterations between the real world and the conceptual world, the latter being our mental model and the former the reality.

The degrees and type of abstraction acceptable to the model-builder will depend on the modelling techniques being used. In a simulation model, the emphasis is on the development of a model that behaves or predicts satisfactorily. Variables that do not detract from the model's predictive capabilities may be omitted by the modeller but be sought by the decision maker. Similarly, if a complex set of relationships has been reduced to a simpler set, then this should not matter to the decision maker. Importance should be placed on the value of the information ultimately derived from the model, independent of the degree of abstraction in the model.

In the case of optimizing models, abstraction usually takes place to structure the problem in a form suitable for mathematical analysis. The assumption of linearity of cost and revenue functions is frequently found in financial and break-even models, despite the alternative curvilinear models used in learning curves. The test of these assumptions involves deriving a result without which the model may be insoluble. If the decision maker receives useful information then the model must be deemed to be useful. If, however, there is dissatisfaction, then the assumptions must be reviewed and more sophisticated models developed.

There is a trade-off between realism and abstraction and the cost in modelling the decision. Models are not perfect representations of reality; there is an optimum level of realism, at which point the benefits obtained from reducing any further the level of abstraction are just outweighed by the costs of achieving the reduction.

Figure 4.1 suggests that as well as an optimum level of realism, there may be a minimum level (x) below which the model is ineffective on the basis of cost to benefit. This reinforces the view that formal models will not necessarily lead to improved decision making. Modelling is not a panacea, but used wisely and selectively it can generate significant improvements in decision effectiveness.

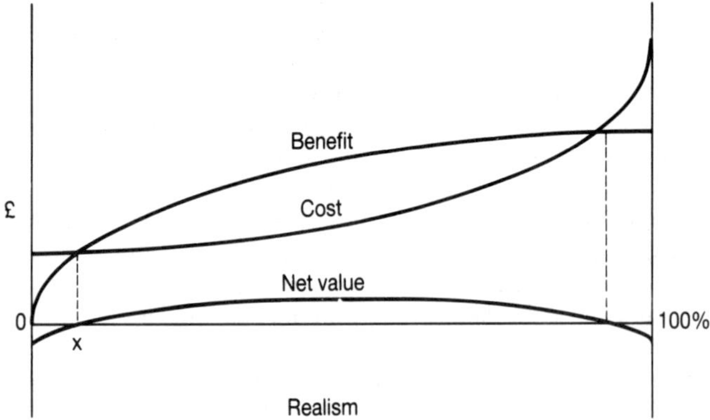

FIGURE 4.1 Cost to realism trade-off

Modelling follows the same principles as many activities in data processing, in that data is captured, processed and stored, retrieved and reported. In so doing, data tend to be attenuated, i.e. compressed. In attenuation, however, the process of variety reduction may lead to simplification that limits the potential of the model, moving from the details of an individual department through to the total picture of the business as expressed in the operating statement. This principle applies in the budgeting process, where we begin with a detailed look at the sales moving through to production thence to department costs and eventually arriving at a profit and loss account, balance sheet and cash flow statement. The outcome of the model, where "what if?" questions are asked, is essentially data amplification. In other words, a limited number of variables interact but produce a larger number of outcomes; this provides us with the variety which we need to make our choices.

The modelling process consists of seven stages:

1. Problem definition.
2. Problem analysis.
3. Parameter estimation.
4. Specification of the model.
5. Encoding the model.
6. Testing the model.
7. Implementation.

We will now examine these stages in detail.

PROBLEM DEFINITION

Perhaps the most common fault in modelling, systems analysis and consulting is the failure to define the problem. While the hard sciences have established formal methods for refining the problem definition, there are still problems of differentiating symptoms from maladies. Soft systems methods such as that proposed by Checklands (1981) provide some illuminating guidance on the process of defining problem cause from effects.

The use of diagrams (Figure 4.2) to encapsulate the structure and content of the problem should be treated as a method of externalizing understanding and agreeing with the client the definition of the problem. The reference to client is to separate the modeller from the owner of the problem or decision. This approach should be adopted wherever possible, to ensure independence of the model from the politics of the situation. It is recognized that all decisions are political, but the model needs to adopt a rationality that can be subject to unbiased testing if it is to be useful.

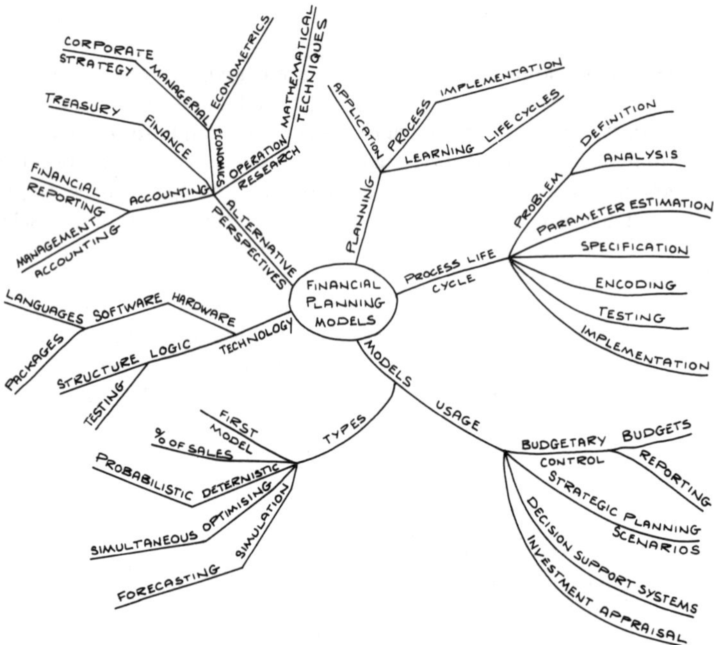

FIGURE 4.2 Mind map of diagramming

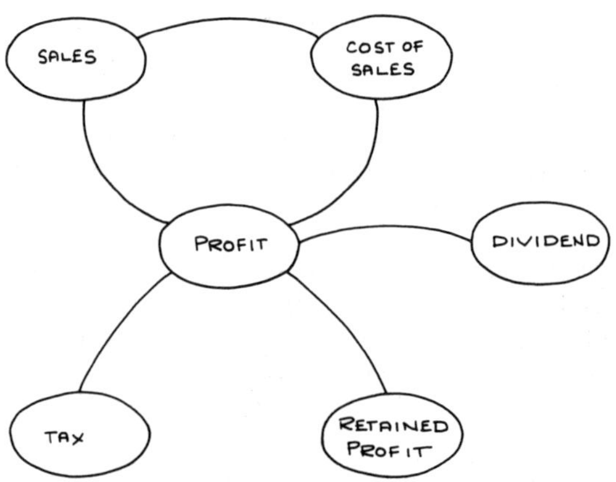

FIGURE 4.3 Bubble diagram

The use of a simple bubble diagram (Figure 4.3) that reflects the key sub-systems and their interconnections with the core problem is a way of identifying the content of the problem. It should be emphasized that the problem must be bounded and that the model may focus on the key elements, excluding by decoupling other complex influences. For example, it is common in budget models to exclude demand. Instead, sales are input as the control variable on the model. This permits exploration of alternative demand levels without the necessity to model demand.

PROBLEM ANALYSIS

Having defined the problem, the next stage is to decompose the problem into its constituent parts. Whilst this is initially achieved by a global view, the major process involves the decomposition of the model into its constituent parts.

The process of analysis is an important experience, in that conceptual understanding is taking place and being tested. Experience provides the modeller with a set of existing hypotheses that will be tested in the new situation. Alternative model approaches may be explored, but the focus is one of analysis and the gaining of insight into the problem situation. An understanding of causality is sought and will be reflected in the subsequent use of the model to predict outcomes.

In the traditional accounting reports of balance sheet profit and loss and funds flow, the mathematical relationships are implicit in the

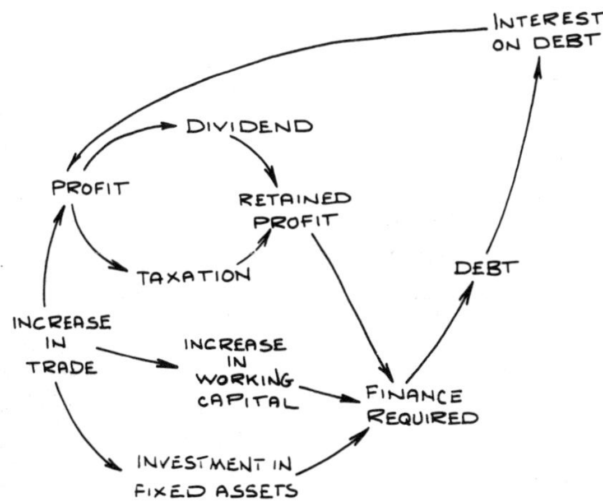

FIGURE 4.4 Multiple cause diagram

accounting model but in order for them to be processed electronically, they must be made explicit, e.g.:

- implicit – sales revenue is dependent on the sales volume and the price;
- explicit – sales revenue = sales volume × selling price.

This process of making the mathematical relationship explicit is fundamental to the computer's operation. This is because the computer will receive instructions of what to do explicitly from the program and cannot assume the knowledge that the accountant possesses.

The disciplines of systems analysis and operational research both offer formal methods for the analysis of the problem. In particular the use of diagrammatic models to represent the flows and activities should be utilized to gain insight into the problem and solution. While highly structured methods such as Structured Systems Analysis and Design Method (SSADM) may be used, more informal methods such as prototyping, bubble diagrams, data flow charts and decision trees may be adequate to gain insight into the process (Wood Harper and Fitzgerald, 1982). All these methods encourage the use of documented analysis and it is this principle that should be developed to allow updating and debugging of the models.

Having established an understanding of the problem, we must move to a problem-solving mode that is akin to systems design. In this next stage we must consider the output from our model, as well as the inputs available, and thereby establish the logic of the process. At this early stage an important check must be applied to the development process. While our understanding of the problem is now forming, an awareness of the feasibility of the model and planning process must be applied. The output of the process and the cost benefit of building the model must be balanced so that the result is both acceptable and feasible to the decision makers.

The information sought from the model by the decision maker must be specified. The aspects of a system's behaviour of interest to the decision maker should be stated and the types of questions for which answers are required should be summarized.

The analysis process identifies the content and influences in two forms: constraints and variables. Constraints are limits that may define feasibility and acceptability. When considering whether to move to bigger premises, for example, the availability of financial resources to cover the costs represents a constraint on the decision. Variables, on the other hand, reflect the interaction of elements of the problem. The constraint was financial resource availability, and the variables were current financial resources, future income and expenditure. An element of problem analysis is the simplification process that will permit modelling. A balance

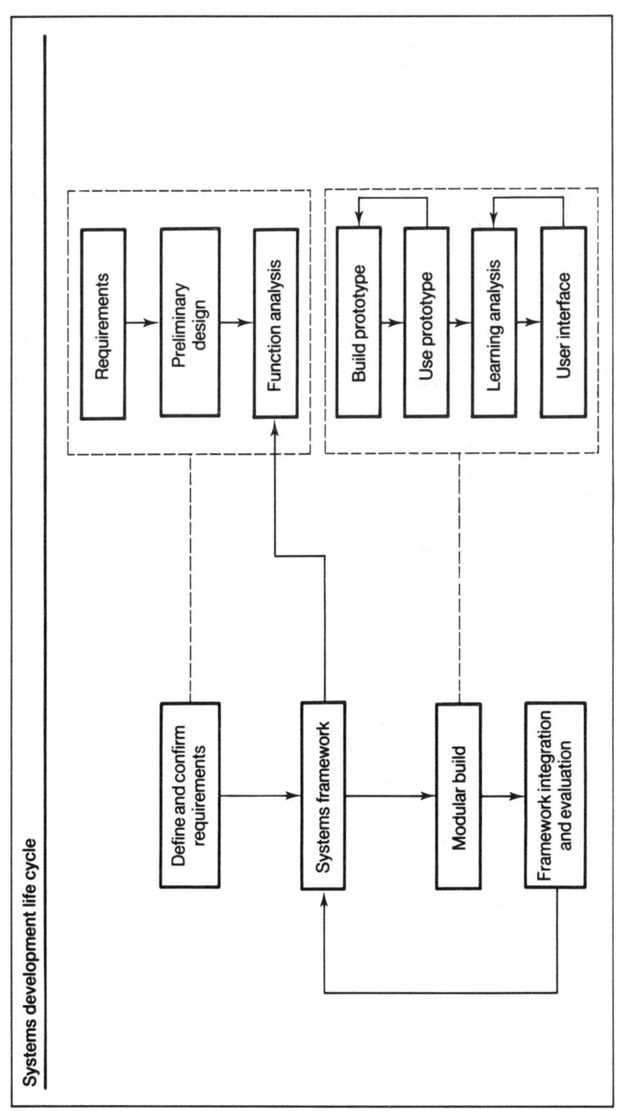

FIGURE 4.5 Systems development life cycle diagram

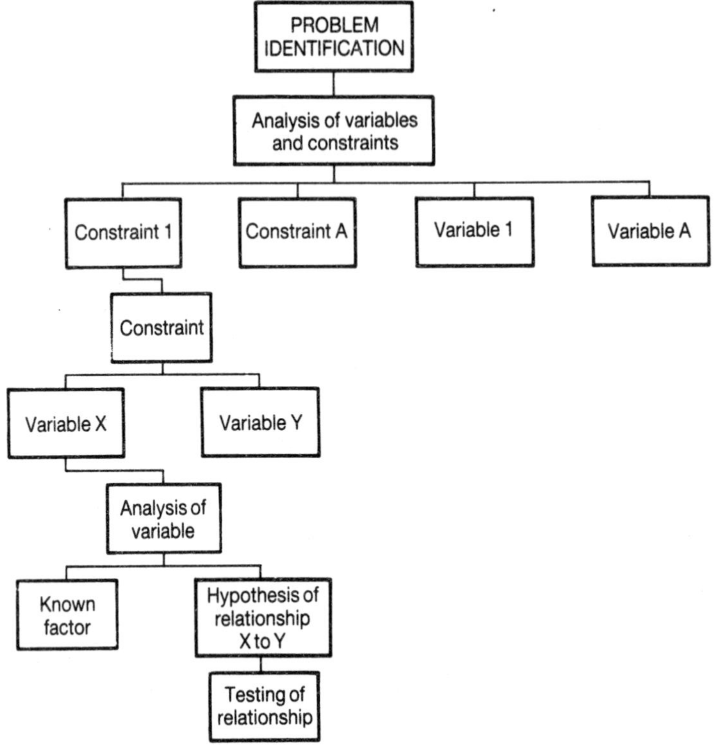

FIGURE 4.6 Problem analysis

between meaningful representation of reality, elegance and clarity of the model structure is required.

The process continues until three characteristics are established. First, the relationships are defined between variables in a structural form (normally mathematical):

Current financial resources	= Past financial resources	+ Change in financial resources

These relationships need to be tested and verified to ensure that they are correct, otherwise the model will fail. Second, variables must be broken down until a known basis, which will allow the entry of data into the relationships to permit calculations, can be established. These known bases may be the existing financial resources (as above), or forecasts of future elements, e.g. sales volume. Finally, the values of any parameters of variables require definition. This involves estimating, testing, and realism. The process is one of repeated analysis into elements until either a known factor is found, or a relationship that has been tested and proved is identified.

The first step in building a model is to compile a complete list of variables that have been identified through the problem analysis process. It should be noted that in the case of modelling packages, a data base will be required which reflects this definition of all variables. It is good practice to mimic this in all modelling situations, to ensure clarity of definition of the variables. Development of this approach permits the definition of the estimate of the variable (input or calculated by model), the linkages both forwards and backward (tree function in spreadsheet auditing), the rules or logic, feasibility range of values, etc. A table may be maintained of this data that may be used for subsequent encoding of the model and to provide adequate documentation for maintenance.

Once the variables have been identified, their relationships must be analysed and made explicit mathematically. These variables and their relationships represent rules by which calculations will be performed to arrive at the outcomes that are sought from the model. The interconnections must then be structured in a logical format so that they move in an ascending order from base input through their relationships to the output. This movement will be constrained by the processing capabilities of the software. In the case of financial modelling packages, where reporting and the logic is separate, greater freedom is available than is found in spreadsheets, where the logic and report format are merged.

Example 4.1 demonstrates a logical progression with statements including input, e.g. price and quantity, for products A and B, as well as calculations, producing results such as those in lines 3, 6 and 7. These are the basic logical relationships that we will use both in financial modelling packages and spreadsheets.

EXAMPLE 4.1

1.	Price "A"	
2.	Quantity "A"	
3.	Revenue "A"	= line 1 × line 2
4.	Price "B"	
5.	Quantity "B"	
6.	Revenue "B"	= line 4 × line 5
7.	Total revenue	= line 3 + line 6

We illustrated the process in Chapter 3, when we developed the cash flow case study. It must be emphasized at this stage that the process of defining logical relationships as algorithms is one that requires accountants in particular to make explicit the implicit relationships that they assume daily. Once the process is begun it becomes a simple automatic exercise. With most modelling systems, traditional expressions of $X = fy + e$ may be more easily understood in the form "Labour cost = labour rate × labour hours + guaranteed day rate." Most modelling systems are capable of testing either expression. However, in the case of the simpler spreadsheets, we may have to re-express the formula as the representative row and column relationships.

Clearly, analysis of the problem and the subsequent identification of constraints and variables reflects the modeller's conceptualization of the problem, and this in turn reflects the modeller's experience. Consequently we find that initial model structure will draw on previously used relationships that need testing in the new situation to establish if they are applicable. If they are not applicable, alternative relationships must be introduced. Alternative model structures should be explored at an early stage. This process of hypothesis testing uses time series analysis, regression and the interpretation of residuals. In this way the interconnection of the elements and their dependencies may be established. An important feature of financial models is the dimension of time. This is reflected in the leads and lags of events from the impact on financial performance; e.g. the lag from sale to receipt of funds. The use of spreadsheet analysis capabilities plus their ability to act as input sources for sophisticated statistical packages eases the process. Additional utilities are available within many spreadsheets to allow sophisticated analysis of time series and other statistical and analytical tools.

In any modelling exercise, one of the first decisions is the degree of aggregation or disaggregation to be applied to the relative elements. An example of this can be given by considering the time element within cash flow forecasting: levels of disaggregation exist yearly, quarterly, monthly, weekly and daily. The degree of disaggregation will define:

- the degree of sensitivity of the model;
- the planning control horizon;
- the degree of variable disaggregation;
- the appropriateness to the task;
- the simplicity as opposed to the realism of the model.

Whilst we may decide that for cash flow forecasting a yearly cycle shall be undertaken, disaggregation into quarterly, monthly, weekly or even daily levels will depend on the sensitivity of the firm's business cycle to trading activities. For example, organizations that are subject to holiday and seasonal business may well find that weekly forecasting may be necessary for highly sensitive periods of the year, whilst monthly or quarterly forecasting may be more appropriate to the slack periods. An alternative approach is to do a weekly cycle to identify critical factors, then a monthly cycle to identify monthly factors, and so on, scaling up. An advantage of that approach is that particular trends may be identified. This would apply to retailing, where there are distinctly different cash flows within different parts of the trading week. Similarly organizations will feel the influence of the weekly payroll and the monthly payroll.

The degree of disaggregation on items of income and expenditure is also important. For example, income from trading may be decomposed into elements of volume, price and payment patterns. These may be further decomposed into: volume according to the number of products or services; price according to the number of price changes or pricing agreements; credit may be decomposed into deterministic or probabilistic payment patterns. A distinct alternative approach would be to say that income from trading results from customers and therefore to decompose according to customers and their purchasing patterns. This may represent a more innovative approach for certain organizations, but probably is highly appropriate where multi-products are sold to multi-customers who, while taking a variety of products in a changing business cycle, may be consistent in their purchasing activities in value terms.

Example 4.2 shows the degree of disaggregation of the cash flow forecasting model we developed in Chapter 3.

EXAMPLE 4.2

Cash flow forecast model

Workings

Sales revenue and cash received:

1. Sales volume = input
2. Price = input
3. Sales revenue = sales volume × price
4. Debt period = number of columns to right shift
5. Cash receipts = sales revenue × debt period

Production and purchases:

6. Finished stock change = input
7. Production volume = (sales volume + finished stock change)/12 (calendarized)
8. Materials stock change = input
9. Purchases = production volume + material stock change

10. Credit period = number of columns to right shift
11. Payments = purchases × credit period

Model

Income:

12. Cash receipts = from line 5
13. Dividends received = input
14. Interest on deposits = input
15. Capital injection = input
16. Total income = sum of line 12 to line 15

Expenditure:

17. Purchases of materials = from line 11
18. Payroll = input
19. PAYE = input (could be made a percentage of payroll)
20. Pension fund contributions = input
21. Advertising and promotion = input
22. Insurance = input
23. Power – electricity and gas = input
24. Telephone = input
25. Postage and stationery = input
26. Rent and rates = input
27. Repairs and maintenance = input
28. Motor expenses = input
29. Capital expenditure = input
30. Taxation and VAT = input
31. Dividends = input
32. Total expenditure = sum of lines 17 to 31

Cash position:

33. Surplus/deficit = line 16 minus line 32
34. Cash B/F = (period 1 = input) (period 2 to 12 = previous period closing balance)
35. Cash C/F = line 34 plus line 33

Note the formulation assumes that the values of parameters may be either positive or negative, and thus the calculation will include the value's state.

The second dimension of disaggregation is time, and the selected segment was monthly.

PARAMETER ESTIMATION

This analysis establishes order and structure on data from which insights and possibly understanding is gained. It requires the use of a variety of techniques, each of which may illuminate a different element of the problem territory. Data can be classified in a number of ways that have distinct processing methods. Textual data can be quantitative or qualitative, but are primarily descriptive and the content may require linguistic analysis. Nominal or categorical data, e.g. male or female can be counted and cross-tabulated. Ordinal or ranked data are subject to scaling, while ratio data are evaluated on a scale where zero is meaningful.

In processing the data the rules of research should be paramount. Verification or refutability of the hypothesis must be possible. Only in this way is it possible to interpret and establish a range of values for the variables. This process feeds back to the analysis of the problem and may illuminate or refute existing beliefs. At the end of the process not only does the modeller have parameters for the variables and their relationship but also an understanding and a reasoned belief in the model(s) under development.

Consideration must be given to the sources of data and the quality of data. Primary sources of data require access and are sensitive to the methods of data gathering, accuracy of measurement, sampling errors and verification. The available methods range from observation, questionnaires and interviews, to installation of measurement systems. Secondary data sources that may already exist may be restricted by the method and purpose for which they were originally collected. Increasingly, financial, corporate and economic data are available through a variety of on-line data services, including value added networks (VANs). These data sources are tertiary and so the circumspection already advised regarding secondary data should be increased, as the further processing of data may have severely restricted the sensitivity and discriminatory capacity of the system. The quality of secondary and tertiary data may be tested by comparison with a primary sample.

The questions asked of a model will usually relate to the values of endogenous variables, that is, those variables that are determined within the system. The endogenous variables will include the aspects of the system that are of interest, as specified in the first step, and any other variables generated within the system during the derivation of the solution. All significant endogenous variables must be specified.

The exogenous variables complete the variables set. These comprise all other variables for which the relevant values are determined by influences outside the system and will be taken to include those variables under the direct control of the decision maker (sometimes referred to as controllable or decision variables) as well as non-controllable variables.

The latter will include not only variables reflecting appropriate aspects of the firm's external environment, but also variables reflecting those aspects of the internal environment that comprise a set of constraints resulting from decisions made elsewhere in the organization.

It will be seen later that the choice of the set of relevant variables will have a critical bearing on the quality of the model that is eventually formulated. In particular, it is important that no significant variables are omitted, since a mis-specified model that yields misleading results could be of less value to the decision-maker than having no formal model at all. Yet while a degree of realism is important, the cost of building a model means that there is likely to be an optimal level of model complexity beyond which the cost of improving the degree of realism becomes prohibitive – where, in other words, the expected additional benefits do not outweigh the costs of elaboration. In fact, the model-builder can usually ensure at an early stage that unnecessary detail is avoided by differentiating between those variables that are likely to have a significant impact on the behaviour of the model and those which represent less important items of detail. If the potential impact of a particular variable is uncertain, however, it should be included because the sensitivity of a model can be tested later and insignificant variables can then be excluded.

The objective of parameter estimation is to establish the value of constants, the gradients or shape of demand and production functions and the leads and lags in time series. To specify the model mathematically we will require the parameters for the variables.

We referred earlier to the modeller's ability to draw on experience of previous relationships, and this may be likened to the engineering or hypothesis approach to parameter estimation. In this approach, hypotheses are put forward and applied to the test data. This may lead to rejection of a hypothesis, the substitution of an alternative, or modification of the existing hypothesis. We could hypothesize, for example, that debtors will lag behind sales or represent a fixed proportion of sales. This process may develop from pattern recognition or derivation of empirical laws such as Pareto, life cycles, learning curves, etc.

An alternative approach is the analysis of historical data through statistical methods to establish causal relationships and the parameters of the variables. Techniques such as correlation and regression may be applied, but it is important to recognize the quality of the estimate as reflected in the test of significance and analysis of variances. The objective of both methods is the specification of the model's relationships.

It is in this area that divergence in thinking exists between:

- the accountant – reporting, deterministic, historic, conservative, implicit assumptions;

- the econometrician – data analysis, hypothesis testing, policy-oriented;
- the operational researcher – quantitative emphasis, data assumed reliable, qualitative excluded;
- the financial analyst – emphasis on monetary unit and measurement, tangible and intangible.

A review of these alternative approaches provides a rich insight into alternative model structures.

EXAMPLE 4.3

Alternative approaches

Definitional equations:
sales = volume × price

Behavioural equations:
demand = *f*(price, advertising, quality, competitive image)

Recursive:
equation 1 → equation 2 → equation 3
cash balance$_t$ = cash balance$_{t-1}$ + receipts − expenditure

Simultaneous:
equation 1 → equation 2 → equation 1
profit retained = PBIT − interest − tax − dividend
interest = debt$_t$ × rate
debt$_t$ = debt$_{t-1}$ + borrowings
borrowings = finance required − profit retained

Deterministic:
profit = sales − costs

Probabilistic:
$EV = P_a p_a + P_b p_b + P_c p_c$

Regression:
$y = ax + b + e$

Logic/Boolean algebra:
loan$_t$ = if cash > 0 then (loan$_{t-1}$ − cash) else 0

Lagged:
Debtors$_t$ = sales$_{t-1}$

Measurement is the process of obtaining symbols to represent the properties of objects, events or states. The symbols, in turn, are numbers or have quantitative implications. Measurement implies quantification, whether objectively or subjectively. It is with the latter approach that it is possible to analyse the cost benefits of qualitative and intangible costs and benefits. Regrettably, it is the limitation of external reporting that limits the accounting practice of valuation and estimation that is necessary for inclusion of both tangible and intangible elements.

SPECIFICATION OF THE MODEL

Once the relevant set of variables has been defined, the relationships between them must be formally specified in mathematical terms. A relationship may be:

- defined, for example, revenue = volume × price;
- empirical, that is obtained by some estimation technique, such as observing the past behaviour of variables (for example, a retailer may observe that the gross margin on sales has, on average, been x per cent of sales value);
- derived by algebra from some other combination of relationships (for example, if the pricing mechanism in an industry is such that a manufacturer's price to a wholesaler is based on cost plus a fixed mark-up, and similarly the wholesaler sells to the retailer on a cost plus basis, it is clearly quite simple to express the retailer's cost of purchase in terms of manufacturing cost and to ignore the wholesaler).

The requirement to express the relationship in mathematical terms is necessary because simulation is a numerical technique producing output numbers from input numbers in a step-by-step fashion. Whether the computations are to be effected manually or with the aid of a computer, they must be expressed in a form that will allow one number to be derived from some combination of two or more other numbers according to a fixed rule. The rule is the mathematical expression of the relationship. The process of decomposing the model is one in which we specify each of the variables and their relationships *on paper* before entry to the computer.

ENCODING THE MODEL

If the model is sufficiently large or complex to justify the use of a computer, the relationships developed and specified must be translated into a computer-readable code and organized in the exact sequence in which the calculations need to be made. Care must be exercised to comply with the rules of the programming language, ensuring that the syntax and semantics are followed. Frequent errors occur due to failure to follow the order of working of formulae and the use of appropriate brackets in mathematical formulae.

In the case of a spreadsheet this involves laying out the relationships within the matrix structure. Speed of calculation will be influenced by the systematic organization of relationships in columns and rows. In addition, debugging and logic-checking will be improved by the separation of data input from logic and the output reports.

Assumptions

The assumptions will represent the input data that will be used by the logic to solve the mathematical model. Alternative data sets will be used to represent the alternatives that are being evaluated. Where choice is not an issue, the use of alternative data sets will provide information on the relative sensitivity of the input variables on the outcomes.

By maintaining the data sets in separate files, confusion can be avoided between the respective scenarios. This is a common feature in modelling systems but may be achieved in spreadsheets by spreadsheet combine functions.

Logic

While modelling systems maintain clear separation of logic from the input and output, spreadsheets encourage the integration that results in problems of auditability and validation. It is essential that the logic is clear and verifiable with test data if the model is not to embody fatal flaws. Good practice encourages the development of a modular approach in which each subsection may be validated before integration into the whole, whereupon further validation is required.

The use of clear mathematical notation and English-like commands assists the building and debugging of models. In modelling systems a data dictionary or chart of accounts is maintained to ensure the consistency of naming and to avoid redundancy. In addition, automatic logic tests are incorporated which provide indications of where the problems lie. It is possible to mimic this approach in spreadsheets by using the naming capability to complement the relative and absolute cell-referencing practice. Recent versions of spreadsheets increasingly include elements of the audit trail of modelling systems and this can be further enhanced by documentary print-outs of the cell references.

Reporting

Reporting is a communications process and it requires the communicator to be on the right frequency to communicate to the receiver with minimum noise along the route and the minimum number of filters in place to ensure successful receipt of the message. Information is received and stored depending on the filter (*weltanschauung*) held by an individual as a result of education and socialization. This filter will guide and restrict the experience of the individual and will therefore determine what information is received, in what form and how the knowledge pool is changed (Episkopou and Kaye, 1986). Traditionally this has led to requirements of reporting such as clarity, accuracy and timeliness. If we wish to exploit modern technology we must go further than this and accommodate the characteristics of the recipient of our messages (Newell and Simon, 1972; DTI, 1990). The following points should be borne in mind when writing reports.

1. The human brain does not cope well with information overload, thus to avoid information overload we must filter and reduce the variety. This can best be achieved by a process of attenuation and amplification, such that the summary report at the front provides the overall picture, but if specific detail is sought then through a series of sub-schedules we can reach a lower detailed item.
2. The human memory at the short-term level has a low capacity of only five to seven digits, so the use of long numbers is inappropriate; wherever possible, we should operate in either hundreds of pounds, thousands of pounds, or hundreds of thousands of pounds. Thus the number of digits to be handled will be reduced. In addition the memory has a large capacity in the long term, but this is complemented by the use of external support systems such as libraries or notes for future referencing. This strengthens the ability to process and handle data. Thus use of a standard format that can be repeated several times would seem suitable as this would permit a return to past records quickly.
3. Current research suggests that memory may be both literal and spatial and this may be exploited by ensuring that the formatting of reports is consistent so that the spatial memory establishes a routine of where to look and the literal one is supported by appropriate explanations and phrasings.
4. The ability to process data and handle problems is restricted by a person's experience and hence the development of experience training associated with management accounting reports must be undertaken. This would suggest that explanations would not be lost in accounting terminology but instead made explicit, thus overcoming this lack of experience.

5. It has already been noted that information overload is a problem in the handling of data, but the actual length of data has been found to be best at between five and nine digits. Furthermore, the ability to judge differences seems to be constant and may be assisted by appropriate supports such as percentages and ratios.
6. Finally, human information processors have a desire for unused data; they have a right to scan and therefore a reporting system should support this approach.

These points argue against presenting a manager with a vast print-out and saying, "in there is some information you might find useful", but it does support the idea of relating data, attenuating and amplifying through a series of schedules like a tree structure.

Further issues arising from these studies suggest that traditional reporting with tables and numbers is not necessarily the best approach, but that rather the use of graphs and pie charts should be considered. This is possible with most integrated financial planning systems since they naturally include graphics packages.

If a report is to have any value then it must be informative, and to achieve this we must consider what is information for the user.

1. *A report must have a purpose* This will obviously be the user's view. Since management accounting reports generated on a monthly basis may go to many separate users, some of whom will find certain sections of the report relevant and others irrelevant, in our reporting system we must provide for multiple users. This requires us to reconcile the conflict of personalizing for individuals while normalizing to a standard format for consistency and to minimize reports and associated work-loads. A way round this problem may lie in providing the base data and model templates to the users, permitting them to personalize their own reports through their own modified model template. This is quite feasible with integrated modelling systems in which data may be maintained in the data bases and manipulated through alternative models. The traditional solution has been to establish clearly by filtering which reports go to which persons, thereby restricting the readership; alternatively, by labelling clearly what the reports are and who should be the readers of each section, a freer system of controlled reading can be achieved. In addition the purpose can be clearly established by defining appropriate headings and titles that inform.
2. *Information has a mode or a format* In this particular case we shall assume a printed paper format, but this may be a table or a graph. In addition the mode may be in the form of a report supported by written comments or simply a series of schedules. Considering the readership and the range of personnel in an organization, this would

suggest that a table of data and a written report that explains the meaning of those data will assist readers of varied abilities in understanding what is the meaning of the data presented.

3. *The timing of reports is critical* Prompt information will permit speedy reaction and correction of performance. This requires frequent reporting of critical items, i.e. daily or weekly and collation of data to monthly format. It is not possible to identify deviations in very small numbers and, as in statistics, one would expect data collected over the monthly cycle would give a clearer picture than one day's sales. This requires a routine that is followed accurately, repetitively and periodically. In addition, the reports need to be prompt to a specific date and this can best be achieved through mechanization. The cost of generating reports is high and one of the characteristics of the use of computers is their ability to generate paper. Currently, studies have shown that, rather than leading to the reduction of usage of paper, office automation has increased the amount of paper output. This can be illustrated by a recent study of one organization that has moved from a report of some 30 pages to one of 300 pages as a result of mechanization. This is contrary to the principles of information overload, however it does permit the scanning and attenuation and amplification of data as required. However, the reader must be educated into what to look on as essential data. The value of reports is closely related to their timeliness, their reliability, their accuracy and their validity. First, one would expect to spend more on reporting to achieve more reliable reports, i.e. less biased for error. By greater accuracy we do not mean the *n*th decimal place, but rather accuracy of measurement of performance, i.e. in control or out of control status. Validity is linked to our first point, namely purpose, since the report only has validity if it is purposeful or useful to the reader. Fundamentally we are seeking a report that gives the trend, the cycles and the exceptions.

TESTING THE MODEL

At this stage, before applying the model, it is necessary to check that it is behaving correctly. The normal method employed is to compare the output produced for some given set of input data against the expected output, probably in the form of actual observations from a previous period. However, there are several test methods available, some of which test different aspects of the model.

It is important to test the logic of the model, as spreadsheets do not have in-built logic tests. The use of a data value of 1 can be usefully applied to test some logic routines, but the manual working and comparison cannot be avoided. Audit tools such as the "Cambridge Analyst" are useful assistants. The inclusion of traditional logic tests such as cross-tabulation within the model are vital.

An under-utilized method of testing the model structure and premise is back-working from the results to input data. This technique can often provide further insight into the model and situation we seek to model. It may be possible to derive estimates of some of the output variables, using other modelling techniques, for example statistical regression. If it is found that the output value indicated by the simulation model is not significantly different from the expected value, the decision maker should be able to use the model with a fair degree of confidence. If, however, there appears to be systematic differences between the actual output and the expected output, then the model is probably mis-specified and steps will have to be taken to improve its design. This may involve changing the set of variables assumed to be significant and/or altering the form of one or more of the relationships between variables. In many modelling situations, the testing process and any subsequent model revisions will be an important continuous exercise. Whenever the system being modelled contains elements whose nature changes over time, it is important that changes in relationships are immediately reflected in the model. Otherwise, serious mistakes could be made as a result of taking decisions on the basis of information from a mis-specified model. Hence the testing process should be regarded by the modeller as a regular exercise, in all except the most stable systems.

IMPLEMENTATION

Having built a model and tested it, we may apply it. However, care should be taken, as a model may only be judged in terms of its predictive power. Thus we must make predictions and judge their quality. Over time, we may gain confidence if its predictive powers are adequate, or seek to revise our model. This process is no different to the development of any other product and is reflected in the short-run and long-run product life cycles. As each model is developed, understanding of the problem is captured and built into the model. The failure of a model to achieve a full representation of reality should encourage the development of a revised and improved model in which further elements have been incorporated. This learning process permits the gradual improvement of validated models.

EXAMPLE 4.4

Development of improved models

Model 1: Profit = sales revenue − total costs

Model 2: Profit = sales revenue − (fixed costs + variable cost)

Model 3: Profit = sales volume × contribution − fixed costs

In the above example, the failure to capture the sensitivity of the model to changes in volume leads to the development of Model 2. Model 3 is the result of understanding the complex relationship of contribution, costs, revenues and profits to volume.

The target of any modeller is not, therefore, the development of the perfect model first time round, but rather the gradual development of a more comprehensive and robust model that reflects the current understanding and knowledge, and which will permit further improvement as additional experience generates understanding and knowledge. It seems appropriate to emphasize that, since the modelling process is a long-term

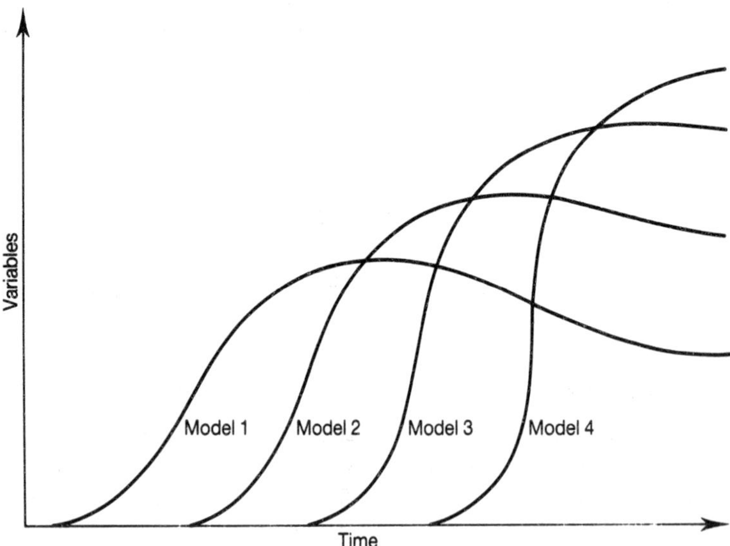

FIGURE 4.7 Life cycle of models

activity through which learning about a business and its behaviour is undertaken, the modelling task should not be seen as a separate specialist activity but rather as the natural activity of management. The separation of the modelling task from management runs counter to the learning process. The learning process permits management to achieve a higher level of control and functional performance. In addition it must be stated that the learning curve promotes support for the view that the investment in learning how to model with a modelling system pays dividends in the long term, rather than the short. Immediate paybacks cannot realistically be expected, nor is it likely to be advantageous to keep shifting from one modelling system to another. From experience, however, the rate of learning a new software system is increased with exposure to a variety of systems, but it must first be built on a competence in one system.

A structural, rational, top-down analysis approach has been presented which owes its origins clearly to systems analysis and design. Whilst this approach ensures a robust, valid model, it can be costly in development time and may fundamentally fail to adhere to the user's objectives. An alternative approach now followed in systems analysis and which may be applied in modelling, is prototyping. Prototyping is the approach in which a model is built and tested to gain experience to permit the building of a more robust and relevant second generation model that more closely approximates to the user's needs. A series of generations of the model thus evolves. This approach is feasible with many modelling systems. It may not, however, be used efficiently in systems that demand the definition of all variables at the initial stage and do not permit subsequent editing. The systems that have this characteristic require a more structured approach.

PLANNING TOOLS

A number of technologies are available for model building. However, the most important requirements for the modeller are:

- a brain;
- pencil and paper.

Without the ability to think and develop conceptual models that can be expressed in diagrams, words and mathematical relationships, we are unable to model. All models should first be developed on paper before encoding on the computer. Subsequent development may be done at the keyboard, but even then there is a need not only to think but also to document thoughts on what is being developed.

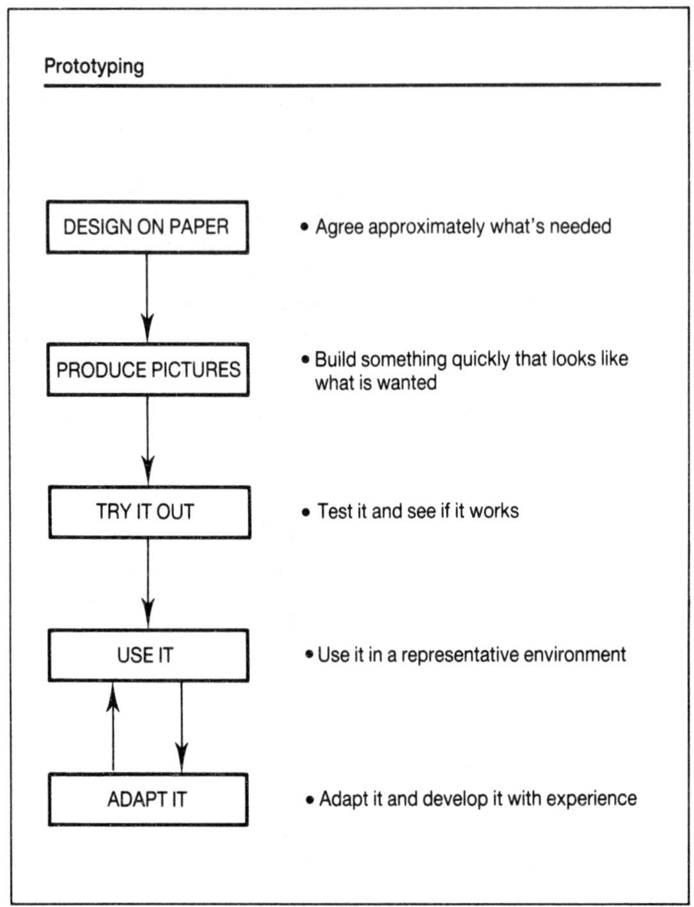

FIGURE 4.8 Prototyping diagram

Most planning and development today takes place in the microcomputer environment, and much of the quest for increased speed and memory stems from developers' desires to continue to run large models on micros, rather than transfer to mini or mainframe environments. This is justified on the relative costs of both hardware and software, but the security and the integrity of micros are fragile and should not be overlooked.

Originally, modelling used to be carried out using a general purpose programming language such as BASIC, FORTRAN or PASCAL. A model developed using such a programming language could take a long time and hence could be costly. It usually involved not only programmers and computer operators, but often operational research personnel and systems analysts who formally defined the problem, the logic and the output requirements to the programmers who wrote and debugged the code.

The first modelling packages, e.g. ICL's PROSPER, consisted of named sub-routines within the programming language that formed a library available to the user as opposed to the programmer. However, the user needed to be skilled and often became a specialist modeller.

The choice of modelling systems is restricted, with some being offered in both mainframe and micro formats, e.g. EPS-FCS. There still remains a need for mainframe modelling, particularly with networked systems, large-scale models, integrated office systems, etc.

With the explosion of the micro-computer market in the late 1970s and the 1980s, a new type of software package was developed – the "spreadsheet". Dan Bricklin in conjunction with Dan Fylstra and Bob Frankston launched the first spreadsheet product, Visicalc, in 1976. This simple grid conceived as a sort of word processor for calculations allowed statistical, financial calculations and cross-referencing within a structure of rows and columns. What they failed to recognize, however, was that accountants had been using such a tool for many years. It was known as twenty-column analysis paper. Unfortunately, at that stage computing power was supplied by the accountant, who undertook recalculation of the spreadsheet when any variable was changed.

One of the classic applications for this manual spreadsheet was the budget. The twenty columns permitted the division of the financial year into twelve periods, with provision for description, variable values, fixed factors and totals, all within the single piece of paper. To achieve greater detail, additional sheets could be used as subsidiaries (three-dimensional spreadsheets) or by attaching together several sheets, large spreadsheets could be achieved. However, increased size led to increased processing time, hence budgets were primarily a once-a-year activity with, in exceptional circumstances, half or quarter-year reviews.

Spreadsheets are based on a large matrix structure in which the cells of the matrix may be thought of as the computer equivalent of a large, multi-column analysis sheet. The accountant has a natural affinity with analysis paper, this being the normal working document, so many found it easy to adjust to an electronic version. Traditionally, the accountant was restricted to about twenty columns by thirty rows on paper, in which data and relationships were expressed and subsequently subjected to calculation in order to arrive at the answer on the bottom line or rightmost column. The electronic version, however, displays on the VDU (screen) only a limited portion of an enormous analysis sheet (e.g. 16 000 cells plus) which can quickly recalculate as data is modified. The display (the window) may be moved around the spreadsheet for constructing, editing and reading results. It may be used for a variety of purposes – not only by the accountant, but also by other managers and functions.

Each cell may have text, numbers or formulae entered on it. In this way, text may be used to define terms, months, sales, revenue, etc. Numbers may form data associated with the text and formulae may take cells and process them against other cells or process the contents of a particular cell against some defined mathematical base. Additional functions allow graphing and desk top publishing of output reports. Most systems increasingly permit interfacing with other systems, such that data may be transferred into the model for automatic processing. At the same time the output may interface with communications systems for onward transmission, graphics packages for visual presentation of reports, and word processing for the editing and presentation of reports.

In using a spreadsheet, the technique is to lay out the matrix, showing workings and reports, entering headings, relationships and formulae, subsequently followed by data that may be worked upon to produce results. A major danger with spreadsheets is that the first outcome is assumed to be correct, when it may contain errors in logic. Subsequent editing and development of the reporting format are essential, as is a process of verification of logic. (In a study carried out in California, 30 percent of spreadsheet models examined contained fundamental errors of logic.)

The crucial distinction between modelling systems and spreadsheets is that data, logic and reports can be separated and saved as files. Models are based on formally stated mathematical relationships expressed in the logic file that may be used in a variety of ways and in a variety of situations. Spreadsheets represent report output systems that will restrict the degree of flexibility of input. Spreadsheets use a cell-referencing system to express the logical relationships of variables. Modelling systems such as Micro-FCS therefore allow the user to run different sets of data through the same logic, and produce a variety of reports from the same logic. This ability greatly facilitates consolidations: for example, where budgets for different departments are added together – a facility only available on the more advanced spreadsheets.

The alternative to both of these is the development of specialist programs. An example of this is the use of FORTRAN or other higher-level language systems. This route has primarily been replaced by packaged software, but it still has some validity, as the building of specialist models may exploit a freedom unavailable in the spreadsheet or modelling package that is constrained by the original design specification. For example, spreadsheets are primarily simulation systems and may only achieve an optimizing model through iterations in a trial and error manner until optimum is achieved. Modelling packages have varying degrees of goal-seeking abilities, but again this tends to be in an iterative manner.

For specific optimizing techniques such as linear programming, a specifically written program using a language such as FORTRAN (mathematically based) or BASIC (general purpose) or their equivalents or specialist programs may be best.

The alternative approach is the building of simulation models in which "what if?" experiments may be undertaken, along with iterations, to achieve an optimal point. This provides not only a tool closer to the manager's own behaviour, but also a learning process in which relationships are understood which may permit the development of complex relevant models of the problems being faced. Eventually this may require a shift to more sophisticated optimizing, purpose-built models.

Batson (1991) has attempted to provide a good-practice guide for modelling with spreadsheets and readers should explore his recommendations. However, we will summarize what we believe are the important features of the tools:

1. The separation of input, process and output. The assumptions are incorporated in the inputs, which are separated from the logic of relationships. The product of the logic is presented in the pro forma report output.
2. English-like and/or mathematical expression of relationships, e.g. sales $= f(\text{price} \times \text{advertising} \times \text{R\&D} \times \ldots) + e$
3. Structured order of processing, leading to accuracy and predictability of outcome, e.g. $Y = p(1 + r)^{n/12}$
4. Provision of subroutines of accepted convention, e.g. NPV, IRR, average.
5. Provision of data base of names or chart of accounts to ensure consistency of usage. The principle of data dictionary as used in data bases should be incorporated:
   CoG: cost of goods sold
   Sales: sales volume
   SRev: sales rev
6. Logic checking and auditability of process and model.
7. Ability to use alternative input data sets, output reports and maintain consistent logic structures.
8. Provision for housekeeping and security facilities. The automated backing-up of models is limited in many systems, with file naming often user-dependent.
9. An easy operating environment with icons, pull-down menus, windows and a mouse (a pointing device).
10. Operating facilities that allow a number of tasks to be performed concurrently and providing a stable interface.
11. The ability to transfer data between various stand-alone application packages.

SUMMARY

In this chapter we have developed a generic method of modelling which is independent of the problem situation or the technology of problem solving. The method draws together the different models we have examined in earlier chapters and facilitates the development of modelling skills that are applicable to a number of disciplines or for a range of business situations. We have followed this method in a large number of consulting situations and have found it commonly practised by other modellers. In particular the practice overcomes some of the shortcomings in individual disciplines and the technological limitations of the available modelling systems. We have found this method to be a way of significantly enhancing the quality and reliability of spreadsheet models.

We have also reviewed the available technology for financial planning and modelling. As we stressed earlier, the technology cannot replace the intellect of the brain. The modeller may use technology to ease the modelling process, but the time and effort in building and testing a model should not be under-estimated. The documentation of the model from the concept through to the coded and implemented system must be retained as an audit and validation trail. The use of pencil and paper and independently worked test data is the only guarantee of reliability of the logic within the model. There should not be any over-reliance on the technology to debug and prove the model, particularly with new or recently upgraded software. The opportunities for "computer assisted error" are extensive with untried modelling systems and spreadsheets. The limitations of existing known software should be recorded and should form a control criterion on the model. For example, one well-known spreadsheet is unreliable with data running to the seventh decimal place. While it seems unlikely that our model would be sensitive to this degree it represents a serious limitation on the application of the package to certain model structures.

The most frequently used systems for modelling are spreadsheets, which have their own particular features that make them attractive to users. However, spreadsheets have significant weaknesses and these should not be ignored.

References and further reading

Batson, J. (1991) "Spread sheet modelling Best Practice", *Accountant Digest* 273, Autumn 1991.

Checkland, P.B. (1981) *Systems Thinking Systems Practice,* Chichester: John Wiley.

DTI (1990) *A Guide to Usability – Usability NOW,* Milton Keynes: OU in association with the Department of Trade and Industry.

Episkopou, D. and Kaye, G.R. (1986) "The meaning of information systems concepts – a discussion", *ISTP* December.

Kaye, G.R. (1988) *Introduction to Financial Modelling Systems,* London: CIMA.

Kaye, G.R. (1992) "Budgeting with spreadsheets", in Dixon, R. and Franks, R. (eds) *IT Management Handbook,* London: Butterworth Heinemann and CIMA.

Kaye, G.R. and Bhaskar, K.N. (1985) *Cash Flow Forecasting,* Vol. 1 in *Financial Planning with Personal Computers,* London: Economist Publications Ltd.

Kaye, G.R. and Bhaskar, K.N. (1986) *Management Accounting Reports,* Vol. 2 in *Financial Planning with Personal Computers,* London: Economist Publications Ltd.

Kaye, G.R. and Bhaskar, K.N. (1986) Vol. 3 in *Financial Planning with Personal Computers,* London: Economist Publications Ltd.

Kaye, G.R. and Bhaskar, K.N. (1986) *Corporate Planning,* Vol. 4 in *Financial Planning with Personal Computers,* London: Economist Publications Ltd.

Newell, A. and Simon, H.A. (1972) *Human problem solving,* Hemel Hempstead: Prentice Hall.

Sherwood, D. (1983) *Financial Modelling – A Practical Guide,* London: Gee & Co.

Smith, F. (1992) "A spreadsheet modelling methodology: its implications for accounting education", in *Selected Proceedings from the 3rd Annual CTI-AFM Conference* 1992. Norwich: CTI-UEA.

Wood Harper, A.T. and Fitzgerald, A. (1982) "Taxonomy of current approaches to systems analysis", *Computer Journal,* 25(1).

5

Building a Model

INTRODUCTION

In this chapter we will examine a number of models to illustrate the generic approach adopted in Chapter 4. We will use the problem of a budget model to illustrate the process, and further examples that embody useful features. In Chapter 4 we suggested that a generic structure for the modelling process consists of seven stages:

1. Problem definition.
2. Problem analysis.
3. Parameter estimation.
4. Specification of the model.
5. Encoding the model.
6. Testing the model.
7. Implementation.

We recommend that you follow this procedure, which we shall use here to demonstrate its usefulness.

PROBLEM DEFINITION

"We wish to develop a budget model for an organization." The definition seems quite clear, but first we must establish:

1. the context of the problem;
2. the expected outcome of the model;
3. the use to which the model is to be put.

We must seek clarification, and in order to facilitate understanding, prepare a prototype model with the user to enable agreement to be reached.

A budget is a plan that quantifies in monetary terms the activities of a firm and its component parts. At its core is the master budget, consisting of the pro forma profit and loss account, balance sheet and cash flow (sources and applications of funds) statement. However, it is usually a detailed plan reflecting the organization, its products, processes and departments. It is prepared prior to a certain period of time, approved by senior management and then implemented as the action plan for the budget period.

The context is therefore budgetary control. The budget model will subsequently be used in two modes: first, as a process of exploring alternative courses of action from which a particular plan is selected and implemented; the budget will subsequently be used to compare the plan with actual performance (Figure 5.1). This control process will require the same structure and data to be used for comparative purposes. An outcome of the comparison may be the revision of the plan. This in turn may lead to the updating of the assumptions in the light of the performance. This would lead to re-use of the model for exploring new scenarios and outcomes. For a fuller discussion of this analysis, see Kaye (1992).

The "master budget" is the term used to refer to an organization's overall budget, which is built up from a firm's subsidiary budgets. Subsidiary budgets are often referred to as "component" or "functional" budgets. Depending upon the size of an organization, it will be divided into a number of budget areas for budgetary purposes. These are likely to be departments or some other units which are convenient for the budget process. The budgets for the various segments of an organization are then built up into an all-embracing comprehensive budget which covers all the firm's activities.

The revised problem definition is now more complex, and requires visualization. At the heart of the plan is the output report representing the master budget, but behind this and building it up will be the subsidiary budgets for:

- sales;
- production;
- plant capacity and machinery requirements;
- manpower requirements;
- materials requirements;
- overheads and expenses;
- departmental costs.

These reports will be broken down by revenue, costs, products, etc. as well as by time (days, weeks, months) (Figure 5.2).

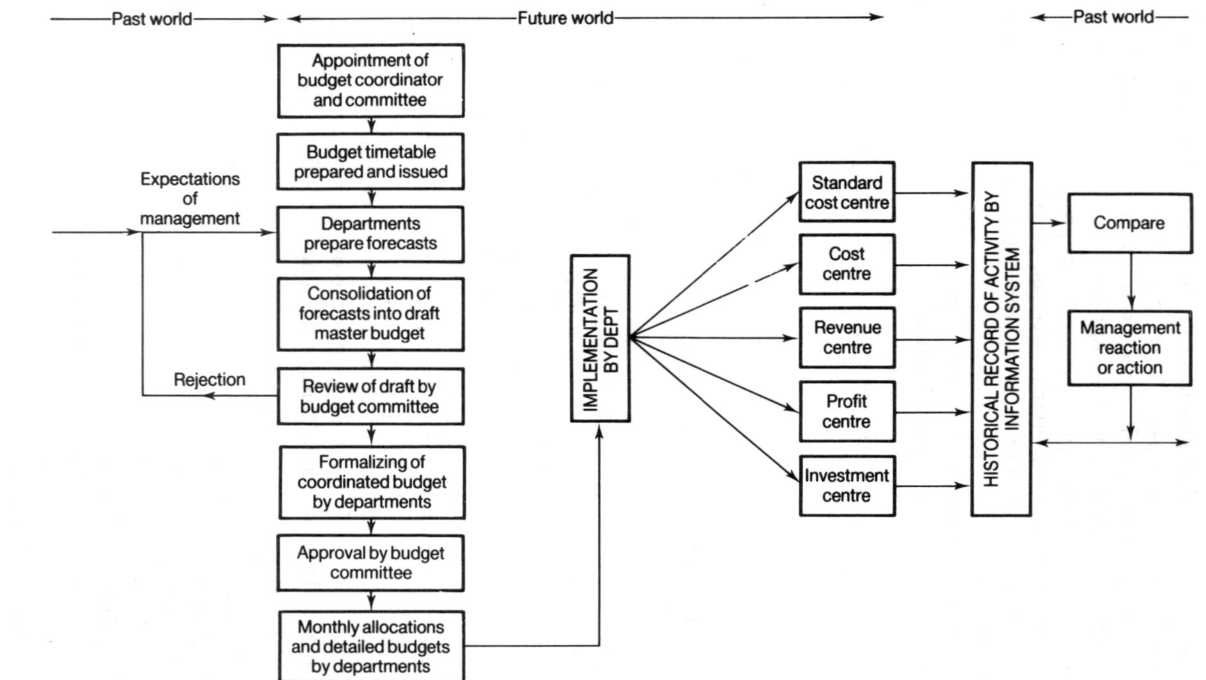

FIGURE 5.1 Budgetary process diagram

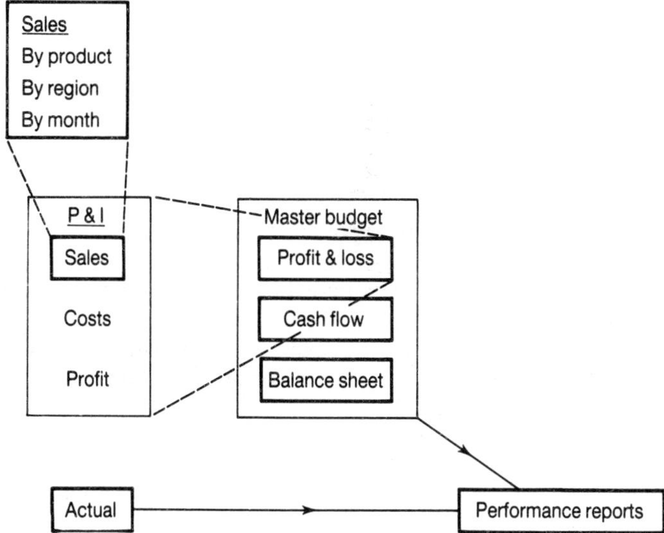

FIGURE 5.2 Budget report structure

Clearly, we cannot attempt to build such a complex structure immediately without a more detailed understanding of relationships and testing. The way forward is therefore to build by increments, adopting both a prototyping and modular approach. Only when a module has been tested is it attached to the main model. Equally the individual modules should attempt to deal with sample elements to prove the structure. The inclusion of the range of products is achieved by replicating the structure for the single product and summation of the collective products.

The key modules are therefore:

- pro forma:
  —profit and loss account
  —balance sheet
  —cash flow statement;
- subsidiary:
  —sales forecast
  —production plan;
- plant capacity and machinery requirements;
- capital budget, reflecting investment plans;
- manpower requirements;
- materials requirements;
- overheads and expenses;

- departmental costs, reflecting type:

—investment
—revenue
—profit
—cost.

PROBLEM ANALYSIS

The interrelationships may be expressed in diagrammatic form, to allow exploration of the relationship and the identification of dependencies. A number of perspectives may be adopted to analyse the problem. First, we could model the activities within the organization and establish their relationships, as in Figure 5.3.

A number of activities and interconnections could be explored in this way. The individual branches can be brought together to explore the network of relationships, but rapidly the network will become complex and difficult to follow. The use of the modular approach will simplify and define the problem being addressed.

Figure 5.4 reflects the cash flow perspective and is a basis for identifying the variables and constraints and subsequently estimating the parameters.

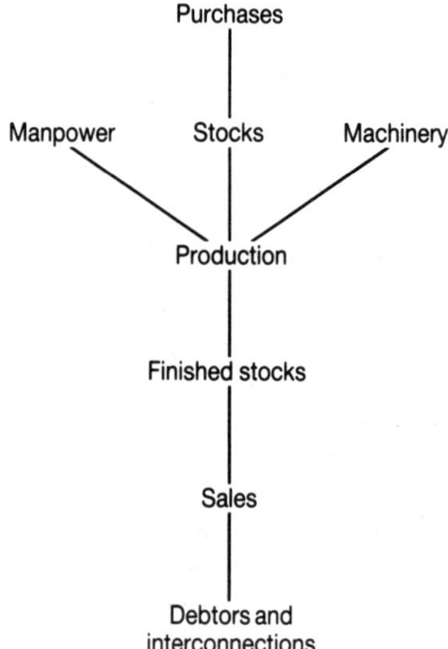

FIGURE 5.3 Mind map of problem

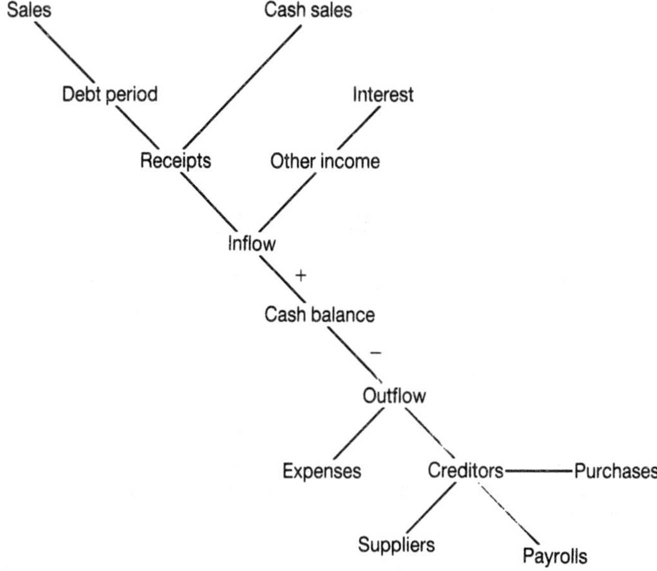

FIGURE 5.4 Causal map of problem

A further perspective we may adopt would be the balances. This approach that reflects the accounting model has been adopted by some accountants and some modelling systems. Essentially, the approach requires the declaration of the opening balances and the model is encapsulated in the subsequent movements of these balances. For example, the balance of raw material stocks will be dependent on the opening position and the subsequent purchases and issues to production. The latter issues will be dependent on the production plan, which in turn will be dependent on the sales plan and finished goods stocking plan.

The outcome of the analysis phase must be the identification of all the variables, both endogenous and exogenous. These variables must be given unique names, and it is good practice to maintain a data table of these variables. In many modelling systems the first task of the modeller is to order the variable names into a data base structure that will subsequently be used for logic testing of consistency. This can also be achieved within a spreadsheet system by using the range naming and labelling facility. The listing of all range names will provide an index to the model, to ease debugging. If spreadsheet auditing systems are in use, or advanced spreadsheet systems such as Javelin, then a tree diagram of the relationships between the variables may be generated. For further coverage of this approach, see Sherwood (1983) and Smith (1992).

EXAMPLE 5.1

Variables and their logic

Variable name	*Location*	*Relationship*	*Parameter/ value*
$DEBENTURES_{t+1}$	C42	$borrowings_{t+1}$ $+ debentures_t$	
$DEPRECIATION_{t+1}$	C17	Fixed $assets_{t+1} \times 0.1$	0.1
$DIVIDEND_{t+1}$	C27	net $income_{t+1} \times 0.6$	0.6
$DEBT_{t+1}$	C10	$Profit_{t+1} - Interest_{t+1}$	
$EQUITY_{t+1}$	C40	$Equity_t$ +net $income_{t+1}$ − $dividend_{t+1}$	
SALES	C3	INPUT	2,200

The endogenous variables will be solved by the model, while the exogenous will be the input data. The exogenous variables are the decision or control variables. In addition there will be parameters of endogenous variables that we may wish to have specified from a table of parameters over which we can exercise control.

There will always be some factors which eventually limit the extent of an organization's budget – eventually something must constrain the extent of a firm's operations. This may be the size of the market, availability of capital or other factors of production, and will generally be found to show itself in one or other of a firm's subsidiary budgets. Examples of limiting factors include shortages of raw materials, labour shortages and plant capacity. Actual examples would include the 1974 oil shortages, the 1975 potato shortages and the 1976 water shortages.

The process of problem analysis will be revisited a number of times if we follow a prototyping and modular approach. The objective of this process is to gain insight into the relationships, to permit the development of mathematical expressions of the relationships. It should be noted that at this stage the relationships are not proven. The subsequent stage of parameter estimation will not only quantify the relationship but also test the tentatively held beliefs from this analysis phase.

PARAMETER ESTIMATION

In this stage we must formally establish the relationships to permit the encoding of the model into the application package. In the budget model we are primarily concerned with a recursive model in which a cascade from the sales forecast through to the master budget takes place. The individual equations are primarily definitional of the relationships. Example 5.2 illustrates the typical sales budget output. The structure of this model is:

$$\text{Revenue} = \Sigma \text{ Product revenue}$$
$$\text{Product revenue}_n = \text{Sales (units)}_n \times \text{Price}_n$$

The logic for the columns represent time periods and the allocation of the sales (units) amongst the time periods is dependent on a seasonality factor, S. The sales of product F in Qtr 1 may be expressed as:

$$\text{Sales (units)}_{ft1} = S \times \text{Sales (units)}_{fF}$$

where F is the forecast of total sales for the year and

$$\text{Sales (unit)}_{\text{F}} = \Sigma \text{ Sales (unit)}_{ft}$$

Another element to incorporate is the cyclical nature of our business cycle, and since our initial model will be built on a quarter basis, we avoid some of these problems. However, in calenderizing the budget and in the building of the original budget, the sales department must identify the cyclical nature of the business activity and reflect this picture to the production so that appropriate levels of activity will be undertaken which will ensure that adequate stocks exist to meet the demand in the market-place.

The overall activities will be defined by the demand pull from the market-place. Any organization has an existing product base which expresses a relationship between the price at which the product is sold, its image and the related sales volume. This relationship is what we require to build into the budget if we are to incorporate a flexible picture of all the elements.

The interesting issue here is where does the forecast of sales originate. In this example, like most budget cases, it is an input assumption alongside the sales price. We would hope that some attempt at demand forecasting has been undertaken and that this has been de-coupled from the budget model. However, for illustrative purposes let us consider a demand forecasting model here. The model below illustrates two features: demand and simultaneity.

The demand for F type products is a function of disposable income, advertising and the demand for G type products. In this example there is an interdependence between the demands for product types F and G (simultaneous). These then are behavioural relationships that clearly require analysis of data to estimate the parameters of the variables. It should be remembered that demand forecasting provides information on the market for a type of good, and not the sales volume of a specific

EXAMPLE 5.2

Budget segmentation model

	Actual	+--	-------	-	-------	-----+	*Forecast*
	---		---	*Budget*	---		
Sales budget	*Prev Yr*	*Qtr 1*	*Qtr 2*	*Qtr 3*	*Qtr 4*	*Year Tot.*	*Next Yr*
Product F (units)	4 000	938	1 250	1 563	1 250	5 000	6 000
Product G (units)	1 100	214	286	286	214	1 000	1 200
Price F	$100.25	$105.40	$105.40	$105.40	$105.40	$105.40	$107.80
Price G	$158.20	$164.00	$164.00	$164.00	$164.00	$164.00	$166.00
Revenue F	401 000	98 813	131 750	164 687	131 750	527 000	646 800
Revenue G	174 020	35 143	46 857	46 857	35 143	164 000	199 200
	-----	-----	-----	-----	-----	-----	-----
	--	--	--	--	--	--	--
Total revenue	$575 020	$133 955	$178 607	$211 545	$166 893	$691 000	$846 000

supplier. The difference will be the market share achieved in the competitive market-place.

$$\text{F sales} = a + b\ \text{price}_F + c\ \text{sales}_G + d\ \text{advertising} + e\ \text{income}$$

$$\text{G sales} = f + g\ \text{price}_G + h\ \text{sales}_F + i\ \text{advertising} + j\ \text{income}$$

We may solve this by a simple spreadsheet and the use of the iteration function (Example 5.2).

At the same time as considering the demand in full, we must also recognize the limiting factors which may exist in production capacity, material availability and our distribution services.

The success of the sales budget hinges on the ability of an organization to make good sales forecasts. The difficulty of making a sales forecast, and the accuracy with which it can be relied upon, depends upon a number of factors. For example, it is easier to make a good sales forecast for an established product which has little seasonal demand – in such cases the simple technique of extrapolation can be used, with some reliability being attached to the results obtained. For a new product, however, especially if it is likely to have seasonal demand patterns, techniques such as market research and test marketing may have to be used to help predict its likely sales. But the use of both these techniques is beset with difficulties.

When extrapolation is used, an attempt must be made to adjust the base of past data so that any of the extrapolated results fit in as nearly as possible with any changes in the environment and other influences which are likely to affect the forecast. Even then, the results from extrapolation need to be carefully examined in the light of information from other sources as a sales forecast model is built up. For example, information from people such as the customer/dealer/agent/retailer/user, and the firm's salesmen and managers can be helpful. Then the use of statistical approaches and techniques such as the use of averages, samples, statistical models, leading indicators and correlations with such things as GNP, levels and growth of incomes, employment and population etc. can be considered. There is also market research, test marketing and other techniques which provide information that can be used to help in sales forecasting.

There are essentially two approaches that we can adopt for estimating the parameters. We could gather historical data and analyse that with statistical methods (see Example 6.2), or we could adopt an engineering approach to explore a hypothesis. An example of this approach is the investigation into cost–volume relationships in the area of break-even analysis. Example 5.3 provides a framework to test cost relationships against known outcome.

EXAMPLE 5.3

Break-even analysis

Plant utilization %:	0	25	50	75	100	110	125
Plant capacity (units):	0	18 750	37 500	56 250	75 000	82 500	93 750
Fixed costs total:	25 000	25 000	25 000	25 000	25 000	25 000	25 000
Variable costs/unit:	1.25	1.25	1.25	1.25	1.25	1.5	1.5
Price per unit:	2.5	2.5	2.5	2.5	2.5	2.5	2.5
Contribution/unit:	1.25	1.25	1.25	1.25	1.25	1	1
Demand (units):	100 000	100 000	100 000	100 000	100 000	100 000	100 000
Sales units:	0	18 750	37 500	56 250	75 000	82 500	93 750
Operating statement							
Sales revenue	0	46 875	93 750	140 625	187 500	206 250	234 375
Costs:							
Variable	0	23 437.5	46 875	70 312.5	93 750	123 750	140 625
Fixed	25 000	25 000	25 000	25 000	25 000	25 000	25 000
Total cost	25 000	48 437.5	71 875	95 312.5	118 750	148 750	165 625
Profit	−25 000	−1 562.5	21 875	45 312.5	68 750	57 500	68 750

A flexible budget may be defined as a budget which, by recognizing the difference in behaviour between fixed and variable cost in relation to fluctuation in the output, turnover or other variable factors such as number of employees, is designed to change appropriately with such fluctuations. Putting this into plain English, we may describe a flexible budget as a reactive model by means of which, given a volume, we can accurately state what the desired level of activity should be in the areas of machinery, materials and labour force, and the associated costs of those activities. From these relationships we are able to establish the relative profitability, given the alternatives.

SPECIFICATION OF THE MODEL

The formal process of specification of the model in mathematical terms is a vital step that should achieve two things. First, it should be complete enough to permit encoding into the application package; second, it should form a part of the vital audit trail and documentation of the model. The lack of documentation and audit trail is a critical source of error and weakness in spreadsheet implementations of financial models.

In this stage we bring together our conceptualization of the model with the problem definition to test the acceptability and feasibility of the model structure. The model will be structured, as any data processing activity, as follows:

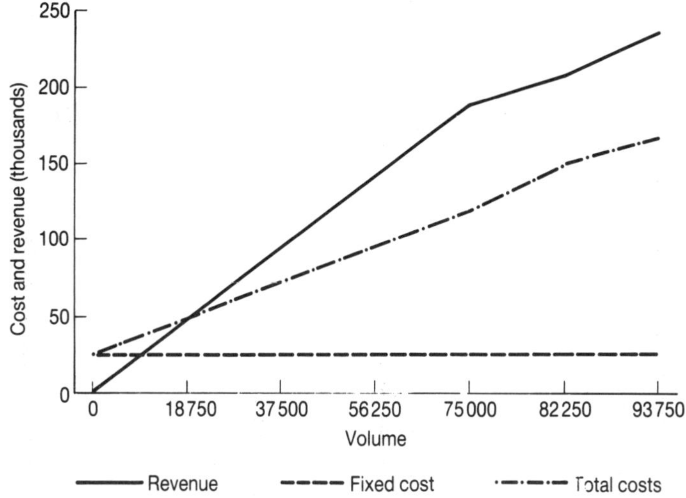

FIGURE 5.5 Break-even chart

Assumptions → Logic → Reports

The assumptions will be constrained by available data and the alternatives we wish to explore. These exogenous variables (sometimes referred to as "controllable" or "decision" variables) will be put into the model and we may choose to explore a number of alternatives by inputting alternative assumptions.

The report output must be in a form which is understandable to the user and structured to form an acceptable report format for either the screen or printer. The fact should not be ignored that multiple reports may be produced from the same logic, reflecting presentation of alternative insights onto the same results, e.g. tabular reports, graphical representation and ratios of performance. The importance of good report design should not be ignored.

The critical area of the model is the logic section that will process the input data and generate the reports. The logic has not only to be complete but must also be tested and validated. Spreadsheets lack logic and audit trails as in-built features; consequently the modeller must incorporate these into the design of the logic.

Example 5.4 demonstrates the linkage and structure of the model, from the input assumptions through the logic to generate the output. In fact this was produced with a spreadsheet in which the label function was used to name variables, rather than the cell referencing structure which is normally followed.

EXAMPLE 5.4

Logic of financial forecast model from Example 1.1

	Input	*Logic*	*Output*
Profit & loss A/C			
	t		$t+1$
Sales	£2 160	Input sales_{t+1}	£2 200
cost of sales	£1 944	cost of $\text{sales}_t/\text{sales}_t \times \text{sales}_{t+1}$	£1 980
	------- -	--------------	-------
Profit	£216	$\text{Sales}_{t+1} - \text{cost of sales}_{t+1}$	£220
Interest	£36	$\text{Debentures}_{t+1} \times 0.09$	£34
	------- -	--------------	-------
EBT	£180	$\text{Profit}_{t+1} - \text{interest}_{t+1}$	£186
Tax at 50%	£90	$\text{EBT}_{t+1} \times 0.5$	£93

Net income	£90	EBT_{t+1} − tax_{t+1}	£93
Sources & applications			
Net income	£90	Net $income_{t+1}$	£93
Depreciation	£80	Fixed $assets_{t+1}$ × 0.1	£81
Operating cash flow	£170	Net $income_{t+1}$ − $depreciation_{t+1}$	£174
Borrowing	£0	Increase in WC_{t+1} + $Investments_{t+1}$ + $Dividend_{t+1}$ − net $income_{t+1}$ − $depreciation_{t+1}$ − $stock_{t+1}$	(£19)
Stock issue	£64	Constant of 0	£0
Total sources	£234	Operating $cash_{t+1}$ + $Borrowing_{t+1}$ + $Stock_{t+1}$	£156
Uses:			
Increase in WC	£40	Net working $capital_{t+1}$ − Net working $capital_t$	£5
Investment	£140	$Depreciation_{t+1}$ + fixed $assets_{t+1}$ − fixed $assets_t$	£95
Dividend	£54	net $income_{t+1}$ × 0.6	£56
Total uses	£234	Increase in WC_{t+1} + $investment_{t+1}$ + $dividends_{t+1}$	£156
Balance sheet			
Fixed assets	£800	$Sales_{t+1}$ × 0.37	£814
Net working capital	£200	$Sales_{t+1}$ × 0.093	£205

Capital employed	£1 000	Fixed assets$_{t+1}$ net working capital$_{t+1}$	£1 019
	------- -	-------------	-------
Financed by:			
Equity	£600	Equity$_t$ + net income$_{t+1}$ − dividend$_{t+1}$	£637
Debentures	£400	Borrowings$_{t+1}$ + debentures$_t$	£381
	------- -	-------------	-------
Total	£1 000	Equity$_{t+1}$ + debentures$_{t+1}$	£1 019
	------- -	-------------	-------

NB An interest rate of 9% is included in the model as a parameter (this will not allow for interest rate changes – an improvement would be to provide an interest rate line in the input area).

The number of periods into which an annual budget is broken down will be governed by a variety of factors, including the industry concerned and its structural pattern. For example, a seasonal production or sales pattern (or both) will affect the way in which the time horizon and fragmentation of the budget is viewed, as will whether the industry uses labour-intensive or capital-intensive production methods. The shorter periods that the budget is broken down into will be the ones that will be used for the day-to-day control of the organization. The overall longer term of the complete budget is more related to the organization's long-term prospects, whilst the immediate shorter periods into which it is divided are about the current situation.

The use of columns to represent time dimensions reflects the vector approach incorporated in modelling systems. This approach can be used to model both time and multiples such as products and processes. The simple replication of logic from column to column facilitates developing the model for the multiple dimensions. However, before replication of logic, it requires testing and validation. This testing is undertaken by including sample data with known outcomes, or hand working of the data.

A further feature to build into the model is the use of logic tests. For example, a balance sheet should balance; if it does not, then the model is flawed. A simple test for this is to include the test:

Capital employed = share capital + reserves + debt

This could be expressed as:

Capital employed − (share capital + reserves + debt) = 0

If this test does not result in zero, then the logic is flawed.

A similar approach may be used for cross-tabulation. In the example below we have used the same logic for the total/sum of quarters intercept:

If (sum of total qtr1 + total qtr2) = (total of sum qtr1 and 2), then total, else error.

In the first case the result is the correct value but in the second case the result is an error (ERR). This is a problem of precision, and care must be taken. The issue of precision is not trivial, as only a few systems provide control over the precision of calculations.

EXAMPLE 5.5

Cross-tabulation matrix

	Qtr1	*Qtr2*	*Sum of qtr1 and 2*
expense A	12	15	27
expense B	15	18	33
expense C	**180**	**270**	**450**
Total	207	303	510
expense A	12.30	15.00	27.30
expense B	15.00	18.00	33.00
expense C	**184.50**	**270.00**	**454.50**
Total	211.80	303.00	ERR

ENCODING THE MODEL

Having developed a specification of the model on paper reflecting our understanding of the problem expressed in mathematical models of the logic and flow diagrams of the structure of the model, we may now encode the model into the software application package.

The separation of the input, logic and output sections will enable debugging and subsequent modification of the model to take place without major rewriting. The modular building of the model is possible if some general rules are observed. First, modules should be self-standing. If they are linked to other sections by dependencies, then these links should be established at the beginning and end of the logic flows to enable coupling and de-coupling. The use of rows and columnar structures enables cross-linking: for instance, the consistent use of columns throughout the model enables a cascade within a column. This can increase calculation speed as the ripples of recalculation pass down the column, rather than iterating from cross reference to cross reference.

The use of simple logic structures is to be encouraged. First, this avoids error on coding, and second, there is less chance of error of precedent within the formula, for example:

5+5/5=? could be interpreted as:

$$5+(5/5) = 6$$

$$\text{or } (5+5)/5 = 2$$

TESTING THE MODEL

Errors are frequently found in models and lead to doubts being cast on the model, modeller and the resulting decision. The frequency of error increases with the user-friendliness of the application, primarily as modelling is accessible to both skilled and unskilled. The ease of building models encourages the building of complex models that are more difficult to test and yet should be more thoroughly tested. The lack of natural separation from input logic and reporting within the spreadsheet family can result in logic becoming corrupted through user error (inputting values in place of logic). The temptation to use a model for a decision as soon as it is completed is a natural desire, that should be resisted until testing is complete. Testing should be thorough and should include the following:

- testing with sample data;
- manual working of important sections;
- tests of feasibility by minimum and maximum outcomes;
- inversion of assumptions (growth replaced by contraction);
- back-working of result to the input values.

A number of quick devices may be used to simplify the testing. In the absence of detailed test data a first trial may be undertaken using simple values such as 3 or 7. The use of a series of simple numbers such as these as the test data makes visual checking easier and simplifies manual calculation.

The use of ranges of likely outcome has been a traditional audit tool and should be employed where historic data provide a significant indication of possible outcomes. This approach should be used at the sub-unit level as well.

The back-working from the answer to identify the input assumptions represents a complementary approach to the hand working and may result in further insight to the model.

Testing will include the exploration of the software application characteristics, which may lead to some surprises. Example 5.6 of an investment appraisal decision generates both a discounted cash flow and an internal rate of return (IRR). However, in order to solve the estimation of the IRR, the program requires a first guess from which it will search. The nature of the search pattern is such that it is possible for a result to be generated which is not the final one, e.g. with a first guess of 20% the IRR is −159%, while 31% generates an error message. Later releases of this software tried to remove the problem but in fact masked it by producing ERR as an infeasible result. It should be noted that IRR is not recommended for use where there are multiple negative net cash flows (Figure 5.6).

IMPLEMENTATION

The implementation of the model after thorough testing will lead to the final productivity gain that the computer model facilitates. The time taken to build, test and debug a computer model is unlikely to be repaid by a single decision, except in gaining insight into the problem. The subsequent use of the model for exploring alternative budget scenarios justifies the development of alternative work practices. In the case of this budget model we could re-forecast more frequently and hence move to a continuous business forecasting or rolling forecast model.

Alternatively, the model may be developed further to integrate with the budgetary control process to enable the generation of variance reports. This would lead to the budget model developed being linked to a new module that brought together the actual result and the budget. The actual result could be drawn down from a data base model by importing the result into an additional input section from which the comparison model will generate the variance reports.

EXAMPLE 5.6

Investment appraisal model

Year:	0	1	2	3	4	5	6	7	8	9	10
Capital outlay:	5 000	2 500	0	0	0	0	0	0	0	0	0
Working cap change:	500	1 000	−100	−100	−100	500	−100	−200	−700	−500	−100
Sales volume:	0	300	600	900	1 100	1 200	800	800	600	500	500
Contribution/unit:	5	6	7	7	6	6	5	5	4	4	2
Fixed costs:	50	60	60	55	55	60	55	55	65	65	45
Net income:	−50	1 740	4 140	6 245	6 545	7 140	3 945	3 945	2 335	1 935	955
Net cash flow	−5 550	−1 760	4 240	6 345	6 645	6 640	4 045	4 145	3 035	2 435	1 055
Cumulative cash flow:	−5 550	−7 310	−3 070	3 275	9 920	16 560	20 605	24 750	27 785	30 220	31 275
Discount factor %:	20	Estimated IRR %:		50							
Net present value:	9332	Actual IRR %:		50.17							
Cum NPV	−5 550	−7 016	−4 072	−400	2 804	5 472	6 827	7 984	8 689	9 161	9 332

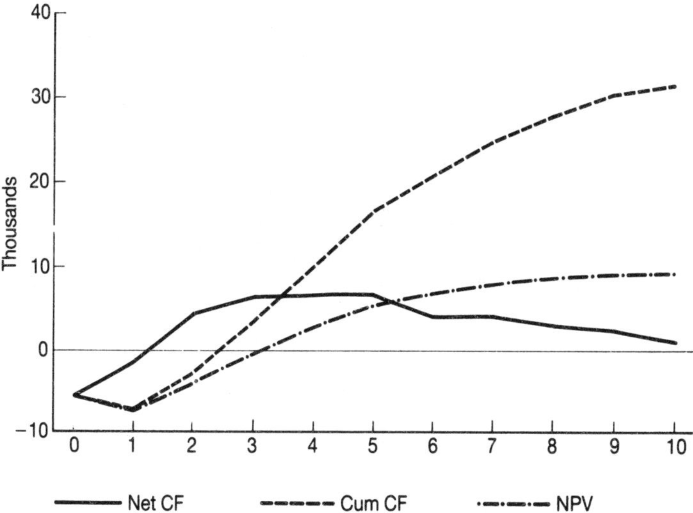

FIGURE 5.6 Cash-flow of investment

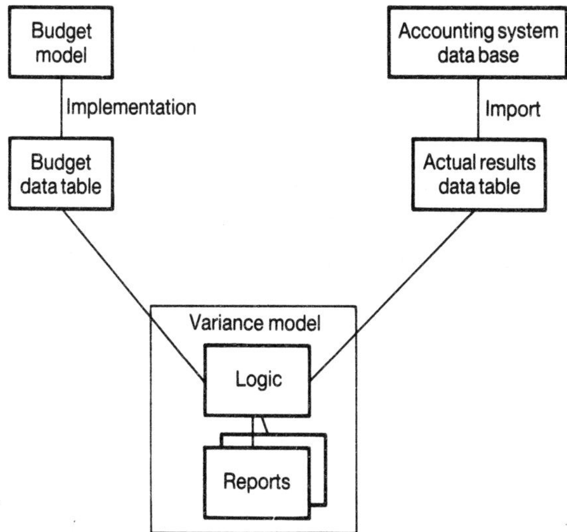

FIGURE 5.7 Structure of a budgetary control model. NB Data tables have been used in this model to provide the input data. In the case of the actual figures, these were obtained by importing the data from an accounting information system.

SUMMARY

In this chapter we have sought to present the reader with one core case study – the budget model. At the same time we have illustrated with alternative structural models that could be incorporated into the model or which demonstrated relevant points. The generic approach adopted is not linear, despite the presentation in the text. There are iterations within the stages that reflect the prototyping and testing of our conceptual model against the real world and the model logic.

It is important to stress that while a model may be built on a computer, the critical factors are:

- our mind map of the problem;
- the conceptualizing of the logic;
- the formal notation of the logic (onto paper);
- the encoding of the model into the language of the software system;
- the compliance with syntax and precedents of the language;
- the detailed testing of the model;
- the learning from the development process and the subsequent usage of the model.

If we adopt this approach our models will become increasingly reliable as we improve them over time. However, we must always remember that the model is only a model, and that reality is never totally predictable.

References and further reading

Batson, J. (1991) "Spread sheet modelling best practice", *Accountant Digest* 273, Autumn.

Kaye, G.R. (1992) "Budgeting with spreadsheets", in Dixon, R. and Franks, R. (eds) *IT Management Handbook*, Oxford: Butterworth Heinemann and CIMA.

Kaye, G.R. and Bhaskar, K.N. (1986) *Budgeting*, Vol. 3 in *Financial Planning with Personal Computers*, London: Economist Publications Ltd.

Sherwood, D. (1983) *Financial Modelling – A Practical Guide*, London: Gee & Co.

Smith, F. (1992) "The use of Spread Sheets in Accounting and Accounting Education", *Account*, 4(1), Spring.

6

Other Models

INTRODUCTION

There are several ways of generating and then exploiting the relationships between decision variables. The type of model that is most appropriate in a specific context will depend on many factors, including the mathematical nature of the relationships between variables, the objectives of the decision maker, the extent of control over decision variables, and the level of uncertainty associated with the decision environment. There are four categories of model that may be applied for financial decision purposes:

- probabilistic/deterministic;
- forecasting;
- simulation;
- optimizing.

PROBABILISTIC AND DETERMINISTIC MODELS

In situations of uncertainty (and we live in an uncertain world) it is important that decision makers gain a feeling for the prevailing risk and uncertainty of outcomes of their decisions. The techniques for modelling this risk and uncertainty that provide insight into the sensitivity of the outcomes are broadly classified as probabilistic modelling. "Probabilistic" may be contrasted with "deterministic" in which single (certain) values are assumed for inputs and thus the model produces single value output data. Some sensitivity modelling is possible with deterministic models through repetition with alternative input data (often referred to as "what if?" modelling, and associated with the spreadsheet models).

Deterministic modelling means determinable, certain or quantifiable. It implies that the outcome of the model is predictable with certainty. Probabilistic means there is a range of probable outcomes for which it is possible to predict with a degree of likelihood; (e.g. 10%, 10:1, 100:1, optimistic, pessimistic).

Model quality lies in its predictive capability. It is recommended that a model is built and tested against known outcomes. This is possible by applying the model to past events. The model may then be subjected to test and development until a satisfactory predictive power is embodied in the model. Once one is satisfied with the quality of past predictions then it is possible to model the future based on assumptions about the values of input variables. The model will then predict the future.

If one is faced with having to model multiple uncertainties, there are a number of routes forward. First, the rule of probability must be applied, that increasing number of variables subject to uncertainty amplifies the uncertainty by expanding the grey area of probable outcomes (see Figure 6.1). Later we will look at some of the techniques that overcome the modelling problem.

Models to deal with risk conditions

The use of the term "risk" implies that the range of possible outcomes can be identified, together with their probabilities of occurrence. Uncertainty implies that outcomes are unpredictable and we cannot estimate the probability of outcome. To overcome this problem we shall assume that all future states can be reduced to conditions of risk. The attitudes of decision makers to risk differ and may be modelled through their risk propensity and aversion. In financial modelling the attitude of the modeller is omitted from the model at the building stages but has to be reintroduced at the judgement stage of decision making. Since attitudes to risk are excluded in the model, there is a need to review the decision from the risk perspective at the judgement stage. However, the design of the model will not be affected by the different attitudes to risk of the decision maker, since the model provides information on outcomes associated with particular actions. Probability estimates will be incorporated reflecting the possible outcomes.

With an optimizing model the situation is rather different. It is possible to explore the impact on the optimal result of changing particular input values. Alternatively one may formally state in mathematical terms the decision maker's attitude to risk and include this in the model. However, this means that the treatment of risk in such optimizing models can

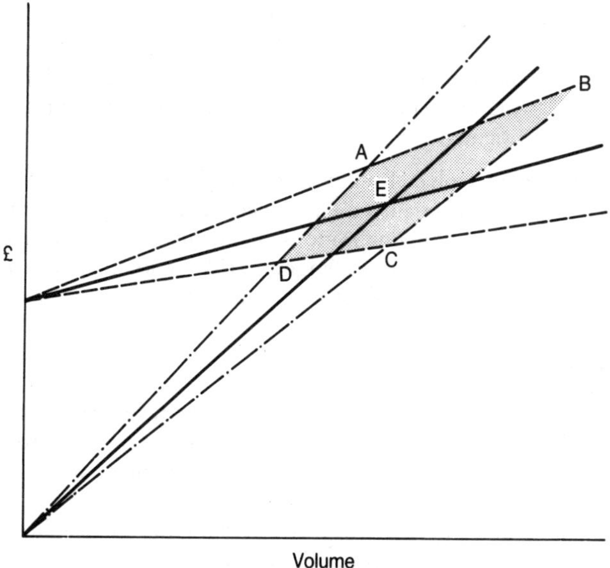

FIGURE 6.1 The grey area of uncertainty of intersection (E)

become rather complicated, depending on the nature and size of the problem and the techniques adopted. A brief review of the major choices available to the modeller is provided in this chapter.

Sensitivity analysis

Sensitivity analysis investigates alternative outcomes with different input assumptions. Not only does this allow the exploration of choices but it also permits insight into the varying degrees of sensitivity of the output, given the different assumptions about input values of variables and some sense of impact of uncertainty. This approach has been popularized as "what if?" analysis that has been made commonly available through the proliferation of spreadsheets.

Although sensitivity analysis techniques do not deal with risk in a systematic manner, they provide a route to explore possible outcomes. The term "sensitivity analysis" can be used to describe procedures aimed at:

- examining, in the case of deterministic simulation models, the effect on output (endogenous) variables of marginal changes in input (exogenous) variables including decision criteria;

- examining the stability of the optimal solution derived from optimizing models as changes are made in the objective function coefficients;
- examining the impact on the basic variables contained in the optimal solution as the exogenous constraints in an optimizing problem are relaxed and tightened.

These procedures involve changes in the exogenous variables, the value of which may be uncertainty. The objective of sensitivity analysis is determining the decision implications of fluctuations in the uncertain exogenous variables. This approach ignores risk, as no range is established in the probability of the input or output to assist the decision maker.

Decision trees

Decision trees form part of decision analysis. The technique analyses the factor(s) subject to risk and uncertainty in terms of a discrete probability distribution. A limited number of sets of circumstances are considered and the probability of each of them occurring is estimated.

A simple form of decision tree is the classification of states of the world into pessimistic, most probable, or optimistic. If subjective probabilities are attached to these states, a simulation model could be built to analyse the impact of risk on various decision choices.

EXAMPLE 6.1

A company wishes to decide its production policy, given that it expects the weather on any particular day will be distributed as follows:

- good (i.e. optimistic), probability 0.2;
- moderate (i.e. most probably), probability 0.6;
- poor (i.e. pessimistic), probability 0.2.

Sales are dependent on the weather on any particular day. On a good day the company will sell 500 hamburgers; moderate, 300; poor, only 100 will be sold. Excess production will be destroyed and under-production leads to lost sales. The product is sold at 50p each and costs 20p for ingredients. In addition, one person is employed to produce the product, at a fixed wage of £10 per day.

The appropriate simulation model requires the sales volume levels to be specified as input:

SALES	= 0.5 × VOLUME SOLD	(4.1)
COSTS	= 10 + (0.2 × VOLUME PRODUCED)	(4.2)
PROFIT	= SALES − COSTS	(4.3)

State	Profit	Probability	Expected value
Poor	20	0.2	4
Moderate	20	0.6	12
Good	20	0.2	4
Poor	−20	0.2	−4
Moderate	80	0.6	48
Good	80	0.2	16
Poor	−60	0.2	−12
Moderate	40	0.6	24
Good	140	0.2	28

FIGURE 6.2 Decision tree

A decision tree (Figure 6.2) can be constructed on the basis of this model to examine each action available to the company. It is assumed here that it will decide to produce 100, 300 or 500 hamburgers, but at no other level.

These output data could be used to determine the best course of action for the company to follow consistently. With the company trading day after day, it appears that the preferred action is to produce 300 hamburgers, since at this level the expected profit is highest. However, in certain circumstances, the company might prefer to produce 500 and gamble that the weather will turn out to be good, at the same time accepting the risk of losing £60. Alternatively, if no loss is acceptable, the company would have to produce 100 and be satisfied with a certain profit of only £20.

The decision tree approach can accommodate as many discrete states of the world as the decision maker wishes to identify. They can be extended to portray situations in which successive events (or states of the world) influence outcomes over time, and consequently the preferred actions will depend on the likelihood of various events occurring in sequence.

Table 6.1 Summary of expected profits.

	Profit (£) if weather is:			*Probability of weather being:*			
Production	*poor*	*moderate*	*good*	*poor*	*moderate*	*good*	*Expected profits (£)*
100 units	20	20	20	0.2	0.6	0.2	20
300 units	−20	80	80	0.2	0.6	0.2	60
500 units	−60	40	140	0.2	0.6	0.2	40

The approach is a useful device for displaying not only the expected or average outcome resulting from a given action, but also the range of possible outcomes with the associated probabilities of occurrence.

FORECASTING MODELS

Decision makers frequently need to form a view of how a variable is going to behave in the future (prediction). Forecasting models assume that there is some underlying process which generates the variable of interest. A model can therefore be developed identifying such a relationship by observing behaviour between variables, either in the past or in other similar situations. In simulation modelling the interest is primarily in tracing the path of the generating process, but forecasting models aim to identify statistically significant relationships between variables and to produce output data that can then be fed as input to simulation or optimizing models. The quality of the prediction is the performance criterion. This can of course be done directly if a modelling system is designed to integrate forecasting models into a wider framework, though this may reduce flexibility.

Fildes (1979) has defined forecasting as "an attempt to create a bridge that links data we currently have with data that we would like to have but cannot obtain directly". Forecasting is used both as a formal technique and as a subjective process of viewing the future. Formal examples include:

- business planning;
- corporate strategy or scenario planning;
- budgeting;
- standard costing;
- investment appraisal;
- project planning and control;
- stock market and shares e.g. futures, options.

The purpose of forecasting may be to:

- accept the forecast and act upon it; or to
- pre-empt and influence the forecast.

This in turn leads to decision making.

There are three categories of forecasting:

1. *Qualitative* Naive methods lacking mathematical sophistication, dependent on judgement by individual or panel of experts (Delphi). Do not rely on hard data, therefore behavioural aspects abound, e.g. last information weighting, central tendencies, bias – optimistic and

pessimistic. There are difficulties in predicting trends upward and downward, particularly as turning points are approached. Does not necessarily build on the past therefore may cope with turning points, discontinuity, technology transfers and leaps. Techniques include relevance trees, morphological analysis (two-dimension matrix of key parameters vs. alternatives), Delphi, cross-impact analysis.

2. *Time series and projections* Uses statistical methods to extrapolate from past to future (time series and curve fitting). Univariate in that it is time dependent. Time series is most useful in the analysis phase of model building. Its importance lies in the pattern generated by time series, not the individual value. Components of time series:
   (a) long-term trend;
   (b) cyclical effects – economics/long-term weather, etc.;
   (c) seasonal effects;
   (d) random variations.

   For instance, stock market:
   - long-term trend (upwards? – inflationary);
   - cyclical effects (budgets, elections, etc.);
   - seasonal effects (sell in May and go away in June);
   - random – (every day).

   An example of time series analysis using spreadsheet to facilitate analysis is shown in Example 6.2. We have three years of consumption data by month from which we shall construct a forecast. Using the graphing function we plot the observations and identify the underlying characteristic as the essential primary step. From this we observe that a cycle exists over a period of four months, from which we will construct a moving average. In order to improve the average we have used two cycles of observation (i.e. eight months). The resulting moving average provides a ratio of average to the actual observation, from which we calculate the seasonality factor as the average of the fourth observation. The trend is then calculated as the average of the moving averages over two cycles. This trend increment can then be added to the previous observation and multiplied by the seasonality factor to generate the prediction. The problems of identifying elements and isolating components should not be underestimated, particularly as cross-effects may be at work.

3. *Causal/explanatory* Involves identifying causal relationships, therefore explanatory that leads to prediction. Most common approach is the use of statistical methods such as regression to identify causal relationships between variables. The use of regression methods enables the identification of correlations, the coefficients of the variables and the remaining constant. Example 6.3 is based on the Lotus spreadsheet regression function that supports linear regression.

EXAMPLE 6.2

Time series analysis

Observation	*Year*	*Period*	*Consumption*	*Moving average*	*Ratio*	*Season*	*Trend*	*Predict*
0	1	1	2 808					
1		2	1 393					
2		3	866	1 896	0.456 630 635	0.409 579 988		
3		4	2 194	1 995	1.099 611 577	1.194 901 924		
4		5	3 458	2 014	1.716 768 028	1.672 483 585		
5		6	1 533	2 036	0.752 946 955	0.732 027 693		
6		7	878	2 051	0.428 136 048			
7		8	2 356	2 027	1.162 165 495			
8		9	3 414	2 015	1.694 397 916			
9		10	1 389	2 065	0.672 598 511			
10		11	923	2 104	0.438 610 039			
11		12	2 713	2 122	1.278 435 53			
12	2	1	3 371	2 135	1.579 200 094			
13		2	1 574	2 157	0.729 548 088			
14		3	838	2 212	0.378 778 462			
15		4	2 981	2 218	1.343 852 136			
16		5	3 542	2 213	1.600 271 079			
17		6	1 450	2 202	0.658 529 662			
18		7	923	2 168	0.425 664 38			
19		8	2 804	2 200	1.274 617 876			
20		9	3 451	2 232	1.546 233 548			
21		10	1 793	2 219	0.807 930 607			
22		11	836	2 251	0.371 390 493			

23		12	2 790	2 267	1.230 565 663		
24	3	1	3 719	2 258	1.646 850 437		
25		2	1 655	2 250	0.735 678 169		
26		3	902	2 277	0.396 113 52		
27		4	2 655	2 337	1.135 950 369		
28		5	4 074	2 362	1.724 992 061		
29		6	1 781	2 395	0.743 477 353	18.156 25	
30		7	972	2 467	0.393 980 848		
31		8	2 855	2 533	1.127 066 371		
32		9	4 447	2 559	1.737 873 089		
33		10	1 936	2 562	0.755 512 195		
34		11	1 023	2 577	0.396 915 466		
35		12	2 833	2 571	1.101 852 302		
36	4	1	4 588	2 541	1.805 766 014		
37		2	1 745			2 559	1 873
38		3	971			2 577	1 056
39p		4				2 595	3 101
40p		5				2 613	4 371
41p		6				2 632	1 926
42p		7				2 650	1 085
43p		8				2 668	3 188
44p		9				2 686	4 492
45		10				2 704	1 980
46		11				2 722	
47		12				2 740	
48	5	1				2 759	
49		2				2 777	
50		3				2 795	
51		4				2 813	

EXAMPLE 6.3

Regression analysis

x	y		*Prediction*
23	12		12.638 772 66
25	13		−13.913 528 59
32	20		−18.375 174 34
43	25		−25.386 331 94
32	19		−18.375 174 34
34	20		−19.649 930 26
45	26		−26.661 087 87

Regression output:

Constant		−2.020 920 502
Std err of y est.		−0.998 185 243
R squared		−0.970 939 098
No. of observations		−7
Degrees of freedom		−5
x Coefficient(s)	0.637 377 964	
Std err of coef.	0.493 140 41	

The resulting equation:

$$y = 0.637x - 2.02$$

Where 0.637 is the coefficient of x (i.e. gradient of line) and −2.02 is the constant.

The quality of relationship between the variables is reflected in the residual unexplained variance. The graphing of the residual allows for identification of any further relationship and auto-correlation. It should be noted that an underlying belief in causality is best tested through these methods (share price movements and interest rate changes) and that a degree of cynicism should be retained in random correlations (share price movements and rainfall in North Wales!).

Table 6.2 provides a summary of the main forecasting techniques with their attributes.

Higgins and Finn (1977) surveying the use of forecasting by British companies, found the predominant techniques were either statistical or subjective:

Table 6.2 Forecasting techniques.

Technique	*Appropriate use*	*Time horizon*	*Technology required*	*Cost of forecast*	*Data required*
Simple linear regression or extrapolation	For simple relationships where the variable to be forecast is believed to be linearly related to one other variable	Short to intermediate term	Calculator with specific functions or personal computer with spreadsheet or statistical facilities	Processing is very inexpensive; the collection of historic data is likely to constitute the most expensive part of this technique	Some past data is always required but extensive history is not normally essential
Multi-linear regression or extrapolation	When the item to be forecast is believed to be related to two or more other variables in a linear way	Short to intermediate term	Without a computer the calculation is very tedious, especially if more than two variables are being considered Statistical package	Processing is normally inexpensive, the collection of historic data is likely to constitute the most expensive part of this technique	Some past data is always required but extensive history is not normally essential
Non-linear regression or extrapolation	When the item to be forecast is believed to be	Short to intermediate term	A personal computer is necessary to cope	Considerably more time is usually needed for	Some past data is always required but extensive history is

	related to two or more other variables in a non-linear way		with the substantial amount of calculation often required Statistical package	experimenting with non-linear models to find a good fit. Data collection is the same as for the other two extrapolation methods	not normally essential
Trend analysis	Forecasting over time in a non-linear way using simple regression	Intermediate to long term	Simple models may be developed on a calculator. A personal computer is required for anything else Spreadsheet or statistical package	Only requires historic data on the one item being forecast but experimenting with trend shapes takes time	Some past data is always required with as much detail as possible
Decomposition analysis	Identifying seasonal components as part of another forecasting method	Short to intermediate term	A personal computer statistical package	Relatively inexpensive as it only requires historic data on the one item being forecast	A substantial quantity of historic data for the one variable under consideration is required

Table 6.2 Continued.

Technique	*Appropriate use*	*Time horizon*	*Technology required*	*Cost of forecast*	*Data required*
Moving averages	Repeated forecasts without seasonal pattern	Short to intermediate term	Calculator or personal computer with spreadsheet	Inexpensive method often used primarily for its low cost	Historic data is essential
Adaptive filtering	Repeated forecasts without seasonal pattern when the nature of any trend pattern may change over time	Short to intermediate term	Simple systems may be developed on a calculator. A personal computer is required for anything else	Relatively inexpensive	Historic data is essential although the level and detail will vary substantially according to particular circumstances
Exponential smoothing	Repeated forecast with or without seasonal pattern	Short to intermediate term	Simple models may be developed on a calculator. A personal computer is required for anything else	Inexpensive method often used primarily for its low cost	Only recent data and current forecast are required as soon as the smoothing factor is established
Composite of individual estimations	Simple forecasting using a large number of	Short term	Very little computation required but	Relatively easy and inexpensive	Past data not required

	individual estimates		processing of a large number of individual estimates may be necessary		
Delphi technique	Aggregates views of a panel of experts and may be used to construct quantitative or non-quantitative view	Long term	Very little computation required but processing of a large number of individual estimates may be necessary	Relatively easy and inexpensive from a computing point of view; however, this technique may be very costly from the point of view of the time required, especially from senior executives	Virtually no past data required other than the expertise of the panel
Simulation	Detailed forecast usually incorporating multiple scenarios	Intermediate to long term	Minimum requirement of a personal computer, possibly a larger computer Simulation package or modelling system	A computer power guzzler; it may be expensive due to sophisticated model design	Emphasis is on current estimates rather than on historic data; however, past data may be required to establish current estimates

	% using method	*% relying exclusively on*
Subjective estimates	73	14
Statistical extrapolation	76	16
Econometric models	44	7
Technological forecasting*	29	0

*Includes: scenario writing, qualitative extrapolation, relevance trees, morphological analysis, Delphi, and cross-impact techniques.

SIMULATION MODELS

Simulation models are the most commonly used form of financial model in organizations. They enable the modeller to obtain answers to "what if?" questions. The decision maker can create a hypothetical situation in which certain environmental circumstances apply, and through the simulation model examine the outcomes. In fact, the decision maker may search for an action that produces a result that can be regarded as being near optimal or satisfactory. Simulation avoids the risks of experimentation in the real world. However, the model is an abstraction of the real world and therefore the prediction is not certain, but useful information can still be derived from even the most simplified models.

The term "simulation model" is widely used as a description of procedures designed to predict, with the use of numerical techniques, the behaviour of real life systems under various conditions. Mechanical systems (such as an aircraft) or economic systems (such as the national economy or a company) are examples in which complex yet stable sets of relationships exist between many components of a total system. In many situations as these, decision makers, whether they are engineers, treasury ministers or managers, need to gain an insight into how the system they are attempting to control will behave under a given set of conditions. Simulation techniques offer the decision maker the opportunity to experiment with a model of the system when it is not practicable to experiment with the real world system. For instance, rather than risk life and limb by building an aircraft first and then test flying it, the aeronautical engineer might instead be advised to test his design by constructing a scale model and studying its performance under varying conditions in a wind tunnel. Similarly, because of the time lags involved and the costs of failure, it is usually impractical to experiment with economic or business policies in the hope of finding the optimal policy. The potential value of developing a realistic model of the economy or a company should therefore be clear.

In general it is a difficult task to summarize the financial area in which simulation techniques can be, and are, applied. Essentially any aspect of business activity where there are stable relationships between variables can be modelled if the relationships can be expressed formally, i.e. be quantified. The following applications are widely used either for evaluating alternative policies, that is testing the impact of various combinations of decision variables; and/or for control purposes, that is determining the likely impact of changes in non-controllable exogenous variables such as tax rates, inflation, etc., when various management actions are taken:

- Company-wide planning models with time horizons varying from less than one year to perhaps ten or more years;
- Functional planning models relating to one part of the organization, for example production, marketing, distribution, manpower planning, purchasing;
- Project appraisal, particularly when a complex taxation system is present;
- Cash flow forecasting;
- Financing policy.

Although not recognized as such, financial accounting statements constitute a financial model of the organization to which they refer. The profit and loss account and balance sheet are, of course, constructed from the detailed bookkeeping system maintained by the firm, and this detailed system could in turn be interpreted as a model. As far as the users of the main accounting statements are concerned, the statements themselves are a model encapsulating the major aspects of the firm's performance and financial position.

EXAMPLE 6.4

Consider a retail company that engages in no other activity than buying stock on credit at a fixed price from a wholesaler and reselling it for cash to final consumers at a fixed price – both at the discretion of the company. The company operates a fixed rule concerning stock levels: at the end of each period, 50 percent of the following period's estimated sales should be held in stock. The wholesaler allows the company the equivalent of one period's credit on all purchases. No distributions of profit are made, and there is no depreciation or taxation.

The nature of the problem here is to examine the impact of varying the price charged for the product on the company's performance, as measured by profitability, and on its financial position.

The relevant variables in this case can be listed as follows.

- PRICE per unit – exogenously determined, a decision variable
- QUANTity sold – endogenous
- SALES – endogenous
- STOCK – endogenous
- PURCHases – endogenous
- VARiable cost of each unit purchased – exogenous
- COST of sales – endogenous
- EXPENses – exogenous
- PROFIT (net) – endogenous
- CREDitors – endogenous
- EQUITY – exogenous
- RETained profits – endogenous
- FIXED assets – exogenous
- CASH – endogenous

Model specification would proceed as follows, all t subscripts denoting values for the period $t-1$ to t, in the case of profit and loss account items, or values at time t in the case of balance sheet items.

Initially the process generating the sales figure reported for each period must be specified. To do this when the level of demand (quantity sold) is being treated as endogenous, a relationship between quantity sold and price must be introduced. Assume here that the company has been able to derive a demand function for its product using a causal forecasting model to estimate likely levels of sales at various prices (see Chapter 7). Let it also be assumed that the relationship between demand and price is a simple linear function:

$$\text{QUANT}_t = 1\,000 - 10 \times \text{PRICE}_t \qquad (1)$$

Graphically this appears as shown in Figure 6.3.

Equation 1 is the first step in the model when the value for PRICE_t is entered as data input for each period. The next stage is to calculate the total sales figure given the price and quantity demanded for the next period.

$$\text{SALES}_t = \text{PRICE}_t \times \text{QUANT}_t \qquad (2)$$

FIGURE 6.3 Linear demand function

Stock levels, as has been explained, are determined with reference to the next period's sales and are adequate to service 50 per cent of the requirements. In general, then:

$$\text{STOCK}_{t-1} = \text{VAR}\ (0.5 \times \text{QUANT}_t) \qquad (3)$$

assuming that the variable cost per unit purchased is constant. The number of units purchased in period t is equal to 50 percent of the sales in period t, plus 50 percent of the sales for period $t + 1$.

Hence:

$$\text{PURCH}_t = \text{VAR}\ (0.5 \times \text{QUANT}_t + 0.5 \times \text{QUANT}_{t+1}) \qquad (4)$$

The cost of sales can be calculated as (opening stock + purchases − closing stock) which, because of the constant price assumption, simplifies to:

$$\text{COST}_t = \text{STOCK}_{t-1} + \text{PURCH}_t - \text{STOCK}_t \qquad (5)$$

$$\text{COST}_t = \text{VAR}\ (0.5 \times \text{QUANT}_t) + \text{VAR}\ (0.5 \times \text{QUANT}_t + 0.5\ \text{QUANT}_{t+1}) - \text{VAR}(0.5 \times \text{QUANT}_{t+1}) \qquad (6)$$

$$\text{COST}_t = \text{VAR} \times \text{QUANT}_t$$

as would be expected under constant prices. The net profit can now be calculated:

$$\text{PROFIT}_t = \text{SALES}_t - \text{COST}_t - \text{EXPEN}_t \qquad (7)$$

where EXPEN_t is provided as data input by the user.

Equations 1 to 7 represent the model underlying a more conventional statement of the form:

	£
Sales (= price × quantity)	*a*

Less cost of sales		
opening stock	b	
purchases	c	
total	$b + c$	
Less closing stock	d	$b + c - d$
Gross profit		$a - (b + c - d)$
Less expenses		e
Net profit		$a - (b + c - d) - e$

Total transactions described also affect the company's financial position. In particular, retained profits at time t will be defined as:

$$\text{RET}_t = \text{RET}_{t-1} + \text{PROFIT}_t$$

(NB: Assuming no distribution of profit occurs)

$$\text{CRED}_t = \text{PURCH}_t \tag{8}$$

Since the only outgoings of cash are in the form of payments for supplies, the balance of cash at t can be calculated as:

$$\text{CASH}_t = \text{CASH}_{t-1} + \text{SALES}_t - \text{CRED}_{t-1} \tag{9}$$

When the appropriate balance for the book value of equity and fixed assets is supplied as data input, equations 8 and 9 correspond to the conventional balance sheet:

Equity	q	Fixed assets	t
Retained profits	v	Cash	u
			$t + u$
		Less creditors	s
	$q + v$		$t + u - s\ (= q + v)$

Example 6.4 represents the simplest of situations. Once the model is encoded in a suitable form for running on a computer, it is capable of providing information to the manager of the company concerning the impact on profitability, the financial position of adopting various pricing policies and the constraints imposed by the assumptions. This model develops a similar structure to that developed for percentage of sales in Chapter 3. Even in this simple case it should be clear that without a computer model the analysis would be rather time-consuming and become quite complex as the number of time periods was expanded and the number of policies investigated increased. The impact of introducing more realistic circumstances (credit sales, multiple products, transactions

in fixed assets, labour inputs, dividends, etc.) would be to create problems that are too complicated even to contemplate without the availability of formal modelling facilities. Simulation techniques can be of great benefit in such situations.

Monte Carlo techniques

Monte Carlo techniques have been developed to make simulation problems more manageable. The technique requires the decision maker to specify the probabilities associated with the relatively small number of (exogenous) input variables (some of which may be interdependent), and the simulation model then randomly selects values from these input probability distributions. The results of combining a large number of the input possibilities and calculating the results will be to generate a representative sample of the pattern of likely outcomes (endogenous variables).

The basic steps in a Monte Carlo simulation exercise are shown in Figure 6.4.

It is essential that the number of "passes" through the model (the number of iterations, *n*) is sufficiently large for a representative picture of the distribution(s) of the endogenous variable(s) of interest to be obtained. The size of *n* chosen will depend on several factors, including the cost of the necessary computing facilities and the number of uncertain exogenous variables. As this number increases, so the number of necessary iterations will increase. On the other hand, as the cost of running the model increases, it may be possible to gain an impression of the distribution of outcomes from fewer iterations. Usually it is recommended that at least 500–1 000 iterations should be performed to obtain stable results, but repeated testing for steady state is essential.

As mentioned previously, this particular method of dealing with the effects of risk and uncertainty requires the decision maker to specify the distributions of values of the uncertain exogenous variables. The relevant distributions may be specified in either discrete or continuous form.

The usual method of generating values of random variables with known distributions is to:

1. specify the cumulative probability distribution related to the original distribution;
2. generate a random number, R, between 0 and 1 from a uniform distribution using a set of random number tables or a random function or subroutine available on most computers;
3. read off the value of the variable from the cumulative distribution.

If the random number, R, between 0 and 1 is generated repeatedly from a uniform distribution (i.e. all numbers in that range have equal

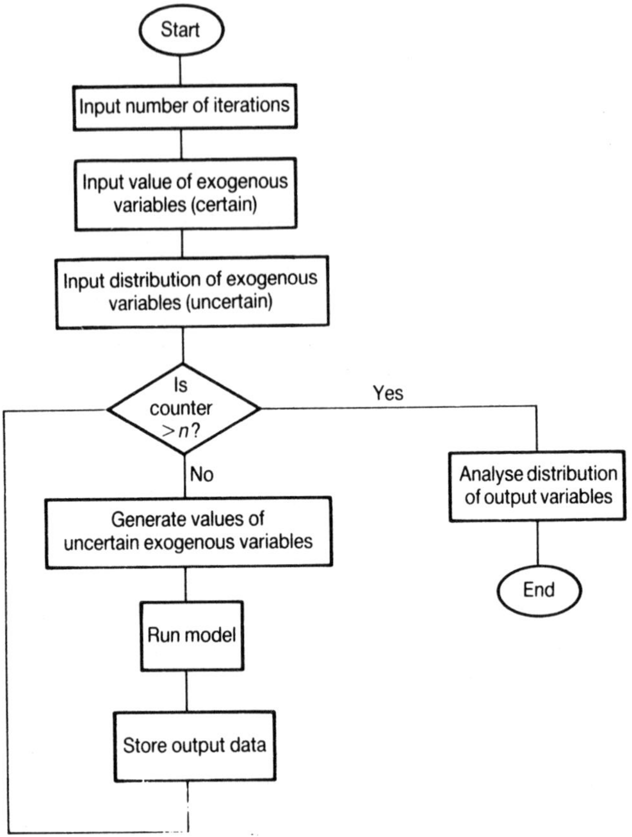

FIGURE 6.4 Monte Carlo simulation

probabilities of being selected), then the values of X or Y associated with R will be generated with relative frequencies corresponding to the original distribution.

EXAMPLE 6.5

If we were considering the maintenance of a bank of thirty machines, and initially wish to estimate what level of service can be obtained with one mechanic, how could we solve this type of problem?

This problem has all the elements of a queuing-type situation which could be solved mathematically, if the breakdown and service times could be expressed in suitable formulas. This is not always true and we may decide to simulate to provide a solution.

1. Determine the distribution of intervals between breakdowns and service. If this information is not available, a study would have to be made. Hopefully, records of the breakdown and repair of machines may be available, from which the distribution may be constructed. Figures 6.5 and 6.6 show the distribution of breakdowns and repair times for 73 breakdowns, and is the basis of the simulation.

2. Convert the frequency distributions to cumulative probability distributions. This is achieved by summing the frequencies that are less than or equal to each breakdown or repair time and plotting them. See Figures 6.7 and 6.8.

   The cumulative frequencies are then converted to percentages by assigning the number 100 to the maximum value.

   Figure 6.7 is obtained from Figure 6.5 and Figure 6.8 is obtained from Figure 6.6.

3. Sample at random from the cumulative distributions to determine specific breakdown and repair times, to use in simulating the repair operation. Do this by selecting the numbers 0 and 100 at random, using a table of random numbers.

   An example is shown in Figure 6.7. The random number of 30 is shown to select a breakdown time of 12 hours. The purpose behind

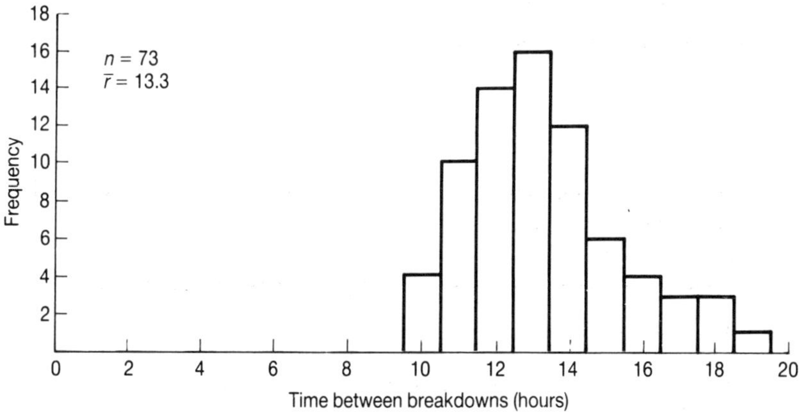

FIGURE 6.5

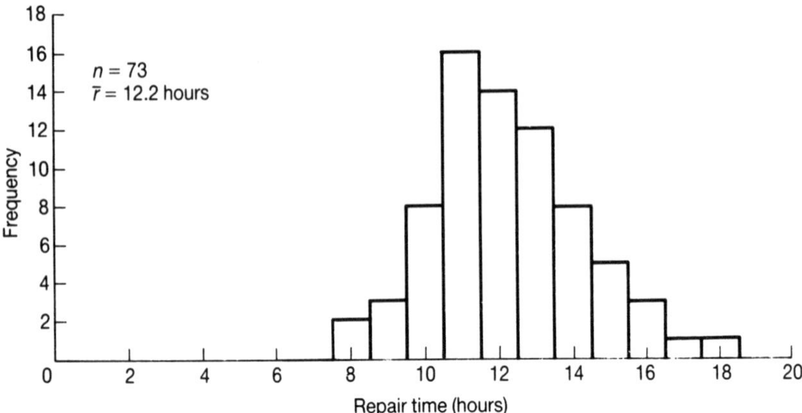

FIGURE 6.6

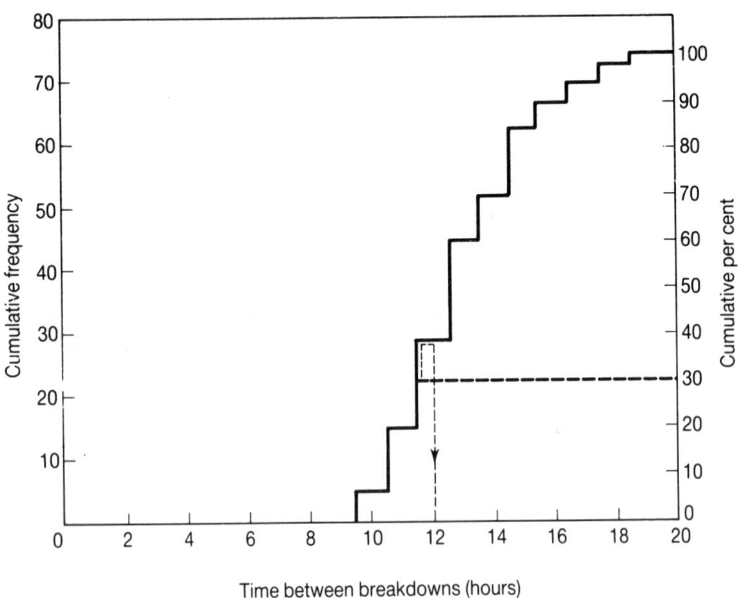

FIGURE 6.7

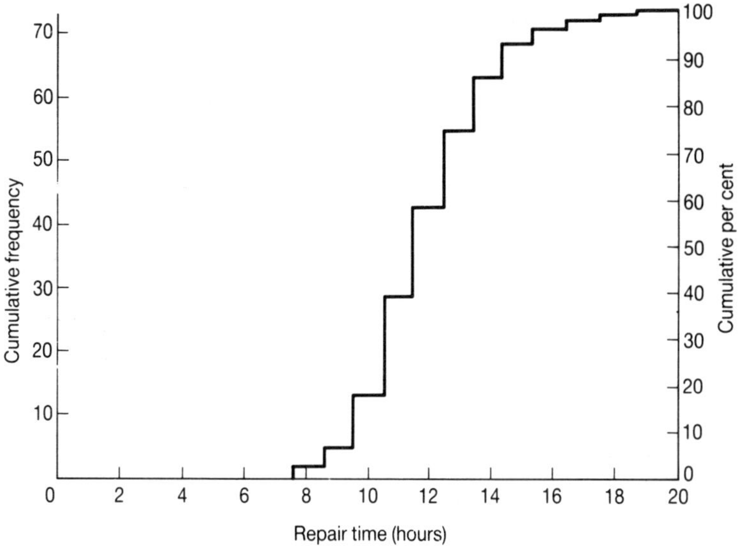

FIGURE 6.8 Cumulative distribution of repair times

the conversion of the original distribution to a cumulative distribution is now apparent; only one breakdown time is associated with a random number. In the original distribution, these values would result from the bell shape of the curve.

Table 6.3 shows the random number equivalent for Figures 6.7 and 6.8.

Sampling using either Figures 6.7 and 6.8 or Table 6.3 will now give breakdown times and repair times in proportion to the original distribution, just as if actual breakdowns and repairs were happening. Table 6.4 gives a sample of twenty breakdown and repair times determined in this way.

4. Simulate the actual operation of breakdowns and repairs. The flow chart in Figure 6.9 illustrates what we wish to do in simulating the repair operation. This will show whether a mechanic is available. If the machine is not available, how long must the machine wait until it can be repaired, and conversely, if the mechanic is available did he have to wait?

   The simulation of the repair operation is shown in Table 6.5. Here the breakdown times and repair times selected by random numbers

Table 6.3 Random numbers used to draw breakdown times and repair times in proportion to the occurrence probabilities of the original distributions.

Breakdown times		*Repair times*	
These random numbers	*Select these breakdown times*	*These random numbers*	*Select these repair times*
1–5	10 hours	1–3	8 hours
6–19	11	4–7	9
20–38	12	8–18	10
39–60	13	19–40	11
61–77	14	41–59	12
78–85	15	60–75	13
86–90	16	76–86	14
91–95	17	87–93	15
96–99	18	94–97	16
100	19	98–99	17
		100	18

Table 6.4 Simulated sample of twenty breakdown and repair times.

Breakdown times		*Repair times*	
Random number	*Breakdown time from Figure 6.7*	*Random number*	*Repair time from Figure 6.8*
83	15	91	15
97	18	4	9
88	16	72	13
12	11	12	10
22	12	30	11
16	11	32	11
24	12	91	15
64	14	29	11
37	12	33	11
62	14	8	10
52	13	25	11
9	11	74	13
64	14	97	16
74	14	70	13

Table 6.4 Contd.

Breakdown times		Repair times	
Random number	*Breakdown time from Figure 6.7*	*Random number*	*Repair time from Figure 6.8*
15	11	15	10
47	13	43	12
86	16	42	12
79	15	25	11
43	13	71	13
35	12	14	10

Table 6.5 Simulated breakdown and repair for twenty breakdowns.

Time of breakdown	*Time repair begins*	*Time repair ends*	*Machine wait time*	*Repair mechanic's idle time*
0	0	15	0	0
18	18	27	0	3
34	34	47	0	7
45	47	57	2	0
57	57	68	0	0
68	68	79	0	0
80	80	95	0	1
94	95	106	1	0
106	106	117	0	0
120	120	130	0	3
133	133	144	0	3
144	144	157	0	0
158	158	174	0	1
172	174	187	2	0
183	187	197	4	0
196	197	209	1	0
212	212	224	0	3
227	227	238	0	3
240	240	253	0	2
252	253	263	1	0

Total machine wait time = 11 hours
Total mechanic's idle time = 26 hours

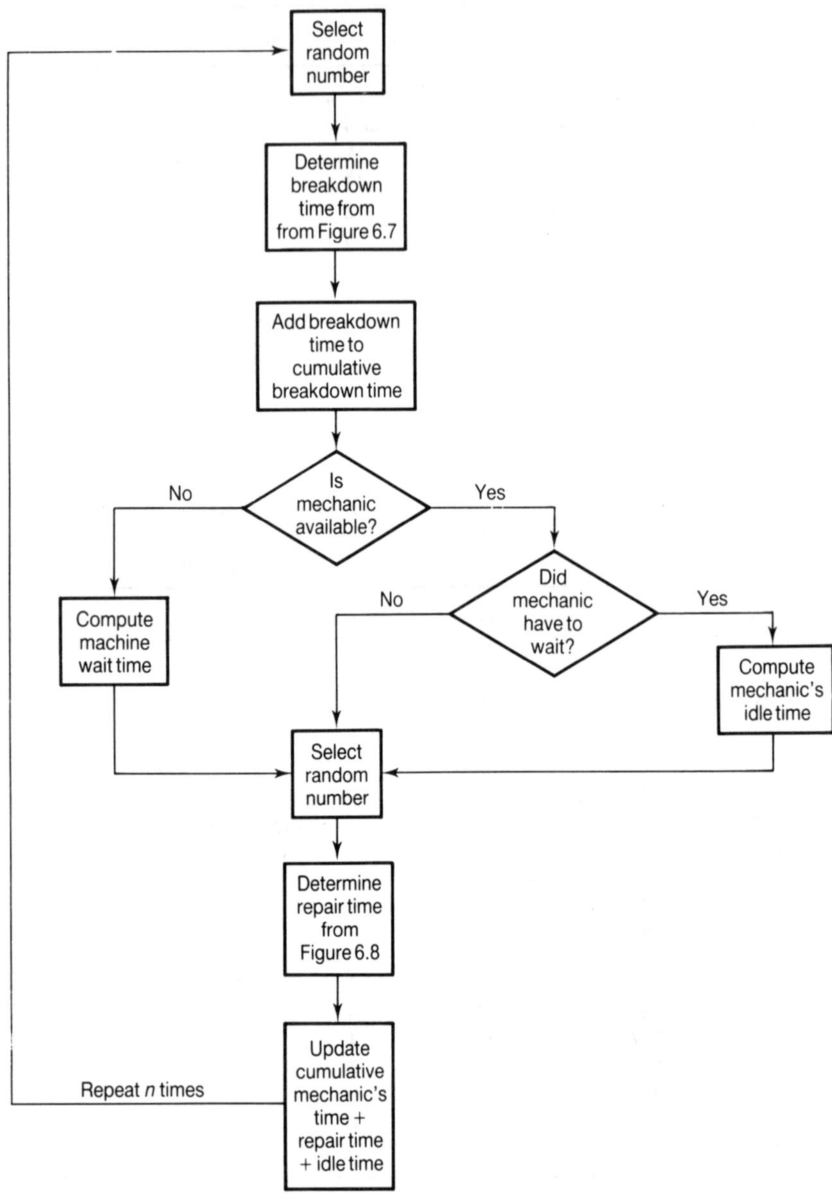

FIGURE 6.9 Flow chart showing structure of repair simulation

in Table 6.4 have been used. The summary at the bottom of Table 6.5 shows that for the sample of twenty breakdowns, total machine waiting time was 11 hours, and total mechanic's idle time was 26 hours. To obtain a realistic picture we would have to use a much larger sample. Using all this data on a computer over 1 000 runs yielded 15.9 percent machine wait time and 7.6 percent mechanic's idle time.

If a computer were programmed to simulate the repair operation, the two cumulative distributions would be placed in the memory unit of the computer. Through the program, the computer would generate a random number and thereby select a breakdown time. By comparing cumulative breakdown time with cumulative mechanic's time, the computer could determine whether the mechanic was available, and if he was available, whether he had to wait. The computations of machine wait time or mechanic's idle time would be routinely made, and the computer would continue repeating these calculations and holding in its memory the resulting values. A large run can be made easily with no more effort than a small run.

When a computer is used the simulation model can become very realistic, reflecting all sorts of contingency situations that may be representative of the real problem.

OPTIMIZING MODELS

Whereas a simulation model affords the decision maker a degree of flexibility in his or her choice of action, optimizing models go one step further in selecting a unique, optimal course of action automatically. The decision maker is required formally to state an objective function, be it profit maximization, sales revenue maximization, cost minimization, or even some more complicated function involving possibly two or more simultaneous objectives. The course of action giving the highest value for the objective function is then found by mathematical analysis. The mathematical techniques used in optimizing models employ systematic solution methods, or algorithms, which can be quite time-consuming and complex, even for fairly simple problems. However, the use of computers has greatly improved the practicability of employing optimizing models.

Optimizing models all have one feature in common: they employ mathematical analysis to discover the feasible strategy (or value of the decision variables) which lead to the optimum value of a stated objective function. The approach should be contrasted with the simulation approach that uses numerical, rather than mathematical, analysis to derive output data and hence an objective function value. Consequently, simulation and iterative search techniques can be used to select only from a limited number of combinations of decision variables the one that best meets the decision maker's objective. The optimal strategy will be identified only if it happens to be represented in one of these combinations. Optimizing techniques guarantee to find the best strategy, subject to the assumptions and constraints defined in the modelling process.

In optimizing, the decision maker is required to formulate both his objective function and the constraints he faces before delegating the role of choosing the appropriate action to the formal mathematical analysis. The decision maker retains the power to veto or make changes to the decisions implied by a maximizing/minimizing model, but any deviation will be around the theoretical optimum. The emphasis is on model specification, since an incorrectly specified model may lead to wholly inappropriate actions being taken.

In practice, optimizing models have generally not been accepted as simulation models in the area of financial planning. The reasons for this include:

- the complexity of many optimizing models relative to simulation models;
- the need to understand the mathematical principles – if not the mechanics – of such models in order to derive full benefit from them;
- the paucity of suitable packaged software making standard mathematical techniques available to potential users;
- the costs associated with model development;
- the unrealistic assumption that managers seek to maximize or minimize a quantifiable objective function expressed in monetary terms.

Despite the reluctance of managers to adopt optimizing models, a considerable amount of work has been done by operations researchers to develop potentially useful models. As implied earlier, much of this work uses mathematical programming techniques, often assuming linear relationships. The main areas in which these techniques have been applied include:

- product mix problems with scarce factor inputs;
- transfer pricing problems;
- input blending problems;
- resource budgeting problems;
- capital investment appraisal under conditions of capital rationing;
- transportation problems.

In addition, other optimizing techniques have been applied to:

- project scheduling problems (network analysis);
- stock reordering policy (calculus; dynamic programming).

Optimizing models frequently employ mathematical programming techniques (such as linear programming, dynamic programming, etc.). However, it is also useful to distinguish between models based on linear algebra and those based on calculus. In the former case, functional relationships can be formulated as straight lines over specific ranges; with the latter, they are instead taken to be continuous. For illustrative purposes in Example 6.6, reference will be made to the calculus model for stock control purposes, the EOQ (economic order quantity) model. The assumptions underpinning its simplest form (described below) are generally unrealistic for the real world; nevertheless, when suitably modified it can be a useful planning tool and is not infrequently used by companies for which the cost of holding inventory is a significant item.

EXAMPLE 6.6

Consider a company using large quantities of a homogeneous raw material in its production process. Apart from the actual unit purchase price of the raw material (which is fixed and constant), the company incurs certain other costs associated with the reordering policy it operates. In particular, there are costs of holding stock, including the cost of working capital, the cost of storage facilities, insurance costs and the expected costs associated with spoilage. These costs have been estimated at £0.50 a year per unit of stock held. There are also costs incurred as a result of placing an order for stock. These include the costs of processing all the necessary documentation and possibly fixed charges, such as transport, etc., and are estimated by the company to be £10 per order.

The nature of the problem facing the company is to choose an optimal stock reordering policy. It is assumed that any policy considered will consist of equal-sized orders placed at equal intervals (the reorder interval) in such a way that demand will be met exactly. It is further assumed here that the level of demand for the raw materials is known with certainty and in this case is 1 000 units per year. Figure 6.10 represents the pattern of stock levels when the usage rate is constant and there is no lead time between placing and receiving an order, with the order size expressed as Q.

The relevant variables in this problem are annual usage (A), the annual holding cost per unit (S), the cost of placing an order (P) (three exogenous variables), and the order quantity (Q) (an endogenous variable). The unit

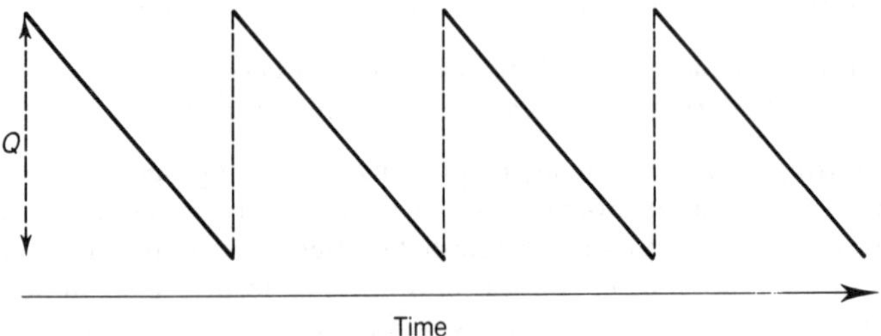

FIGURE 6.10 Pattern of stock levels

cost of raw material stock is also exogenous, but irrelevant, since the total purchase cost will be the same whatever reorder policy is adopted (cash flow considerations, discounts, and so on, are ignored here).

The objective function can now be formulated for the relevant variables.

Minimize total costs = holding costs + total ordering costs
= (average stock level × unit holding cost per annum)
+ (number of orders × cost of placing order)

$$= \left(\frac{Q}{2} \times S\right) + \left(\frac{A}{Q} \times P\right) + \frac{QS}{2} + \frac{AP}{Q} \tag{10}$$

In this simple example there are no constraints, except that the order quantity should be a positive number. The difficulty for the decision maker is in determining the optimal value for Q, i.e. that value that minimizes total costs.

Diagrammatically, the problem can be expressed as shown in Figure 6.11.

In this case it is easiest to determine the optimal solution using elementary calculus, although it is not strictly necessary since it can be argued that the optimal order quantity is where the incremental cost of holding stock is no greater than the cost of ordering, i.e. Q is optimal where

$$\frac{QS}{2} = \frac{AP}{Q} \tag{11}$$

from which it is obvious

$$Q^2S = 2AP \tag{12}$$

$$Q = \sqrt{\frac{2AP}{S}} \tag{13}$$

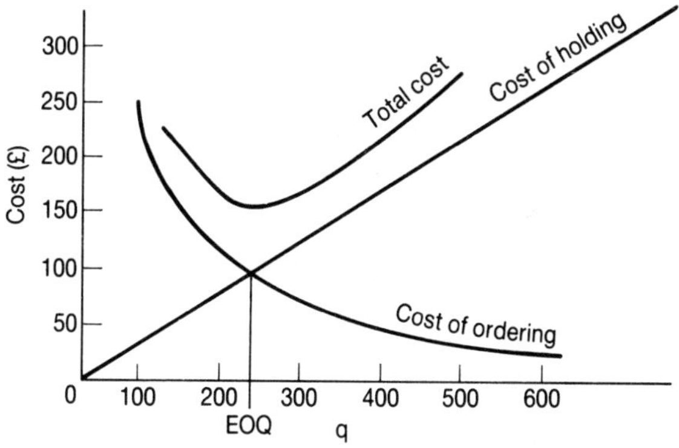

FIGURE 6.11 Stock holding and ordering costs and EOQ

The same result can be derived by calculus, by differentiating the function with respect to the decision variable and setting the result to zero. Expressed formally:

$$\frac{d(TC)}{dQ} = \frac{S}{2} - \frac{AP}{Q^2} = 0 \qquad (14)$$

therefore

$$Q^2 = \frac{2AP}{S} \qquad (15)$$

or

$$Q = \sqrt{\frac{2AP}{S}} \qquad (13)$$

Equation 13 is the general solution for the volume of Q that minimizes total cost (equation 10). Strictly speaking, we should check that a minimum point has been found, and not a maximum, by differentiating a second time and checking the sign of the resulting expression:

$$\frac{d^2(TC)}{dQ^2} = \frac{2AP}{Q^3} > 0 \text{ since } A,\ P,\ Q \text{ r1 } 0$$

Therefore a minimum point exists when Q is defined as in expression 13. This is the general solution, and in the specific example introduced above the optimal solution for Q could be found in two ways – by substituting the values of *A*, *P* and *S* in equation 10.

SUMMARY

In this chapter we have sought to provide a range of models and modelling techniques with which we can develop our financial plans. The difficulty a modeller faces in handling risk and uncertainty was alluded to at the beginning of the chapter. Solutions to the problem of modelling uncertainty, include:

- fragment the model and isolate the uncertainties in separate models;
- use decision trees to develop linked structures: (powerful for sequential models – if A, then B or C);
- simulate until steady state using Monte Carlo methods;
- increase the hurdle criteria or rates (DCF) to cover riskiness;
- adjust the utility (contribution) to cover the risky element;
- develop a distribution model that provides a range of outcomes with associated map of uncertainty.

Many of these techniques require formal methods and we would recommend that you adopt the methods developed in Chapter 4. In addition, many of these models required a computer to solve them and avoid laborious manual calculation. In our final chapter we will consider some of the technology choices we have to make in planning and building models.

References and further reading

Bhaskar, K.N. (1978) *Building Financial Models – A Simulation Approach,* London: Associated Business Press.

Bridges, J. (1989) *Managerial Decisions with the Microcomputer,* Hemel Hempstead: Philip Allan.

Chambers, J.O., Mullick, S.K. and Smith, D.D. (1971) "How do we choose the right forecasting technique", *Harvard Business Review,* July/August.

Cretein, P.D., Ball, S.E. and Brigham, E.F. (1987) *Financial Management using Lotus 1-2-3,* New York: Dryden Press.

Fildes, R. (1979) "Quantitative Forecasting – The state of the art: extrapolative models", *Journal of Operational Research Quarterly,* 30(8), August.

Higgins, J.C. (1980) *Strategic and Operational Planning Systems – Principles and Practice,* Hemel Hempstead: Prentice Hall.

Higgins, J.C. and Finn, R. (1977) *Planning models in the UK: A survey,* Omega, Vol No. 2.

Jackson, M. (1988) *Creative Modelling with Lotus 1-2-3,* Chichester: John Wiley.

Jackson, M. (1988) *Advanced Spreadsheet Modelling with Lotus 1-2-3,* Chichester: John Wiley.

Koutsoyiannis, A. (1986) *Theory on Econometrics,* (2nd edn). Basingstoke: Macmillan.

Kyd Osborne, C.W. (1986) *Financial Modelling using Lotus 1-2-3,* Maidenhead: McGraw Hill.

Lewis, C. (1989) *Business Forecasting in a Lotus 1-2-3 Environment.* Chichester: John Wiley.

Mendeenhall, W., Reinmuth, J.E., Beaver, R. and Dunman, D. (1982) *Statistics for Management and Economics,* Duxbury Press.

Naylor, T.H., Vernon, J.M. and Wertz, K.L. (1983) *Managerial Economics,* Maidenhead: McGraw Hill.

Remenyi, D. and Nugus, S. (1988) *Business Applications in Lotus 1-2-3: A Guide to Forecasting, Risk Analysis, Backward Iterations and Simulation,* Maidenhead: McGraw Hill.

Schlosser, M. (1989) *Corporate Finance,* Hemel Hempstead: Prentice Hall.

Sherwood, D. (1983) *Financial Modelling Practical Guide,* London: Gee & Co.

Taha, H.A. (1987) *Operational Research,* Basingstoke: Macmillan.

7

Modelling and Decision Support Systems

INTRODUCTION

A traditional classification of management activity encompasses the following categories:

- planning;
- control;
- decision making;
- motivation;
- co-ordination.

The process of planning and control are arguably inseparable. Decision making is primarily the task of management, whether for routine or *ad hoc* events. Motivation and co-ordination reflect the importance of the behavioural dimension in ensuring that management's intentions are implemented by others. This later perspective cannot easily be modelled and hence is often omitted from models, undermining their predictive capabilities.

Gilligan, Neale and Murray (1983) suggest that a decision cycle exists which links the elements together, from the plan embodied in the objective to the decision and the subsequent control. To this end, management science has developed techniques to support decision making, which form the tools of modelling:

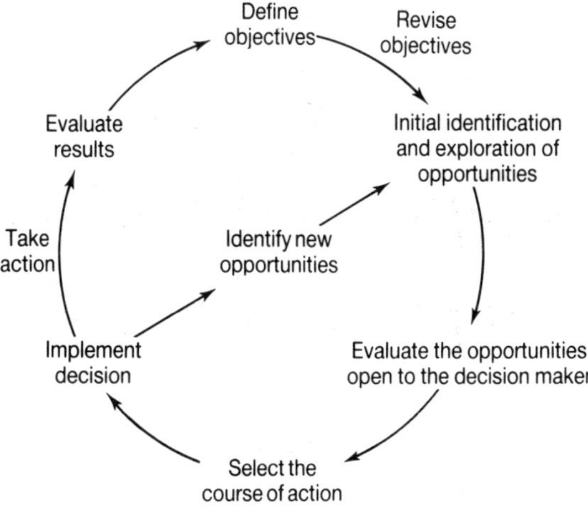

FIGURE 7.1 Decision cycle

- probability;
- decision theory;
- linear programming;
- economic order quantity;
- Pareto analysis;
- discounted cash flow;
- network analysis;
- simulation.

Many of these techniques exploit computers to solve the mathematics and a range of application packages has been developed to support this work (Plane, 1986). These application packages are the founding fathers of modelling systems, embodying the development of sub-routines for model building.

The term "decision support systems" (DSSs), which describes computer-based analytical aid to decision making, was coined way back in 1970 by Peter Keen. The early developers who were concerned with integration of quantitative techniques with computers were restricted to programming languages and mainframe computers that were unlikely to support the inexpert user. A historical progression exists in the development of information systems, from data processing, through management information systems to expert systems and executive information systems. A key difference between DSSs and DP (data processing) was the interaction with the end user, typically a manager using the computer system without assistance or formal training. The system would therefore be "user friendly".

The recognition of the importance of the task context and organizational positioning and behaviour was not ignored by these developers, but the available tools at that time severely restricted their capacity to deliver generalizable systems. Consequently DSSs in the 1970s and 1980s were restricted to specific tasks and organizational situations.

With the proliferation of personal computers, user friendliness has become the norm, but DSSs have remained essentially associated with operational research techniques, including linear programming and modelling. Recently, there has been a move back to DSSs as a result of the linking of corporate data bases with personal computers using local area networks and wide area networks communication systems. This has permitted the available data to be processed through a variety of user-friendly, micro-based packages from linear programming, statistical analysis, etc. to established modelling systems. Some of these packages have their origin in cumbersome mainframe systems that, when revised to fit a micro, have been given completely new user interfaces. Others are entirely new systems.

Alter (1977) suggested the following taxonomy of decision support systems:

- the filing cabinet;
- data analysis systems;
- data bases and small models;
- accounting models;
- representational models;
- optimizing models;
- suggestion models.

While the lowest forms of DSS may be described as the systematic storage of data by file structures to enable ease of retrieval, the development of data bases reflects advances in data processing to enable hierarchical as well as relative retrieval of data. The development of accounting models reflects the convergence of information processing systems from data processing with theoretical frameworks of knowledge and understanding. The subsequent development of higher level models exploits the management sciences to support rational decision making. However, the final category reflects the incorporation of intelligence and experience and may be seen in expert systems and the application of neural networks to problem solving with complex data. These later systems incorporate not only data but knowledge, represented by rules and evidence.

MANAGEMENT ACCOUNTING SUPPORTS

A business model offers management one of the most powerful techniques for business planning; it is sometimes referred to as a decision support system. A business model allows management to test out the implications of their plans, strategies and tactics on the business without committing the company either to expensive experiments (toe-testing) or to irreversible steps into the unknown. This is achieved by producing alternative plans and testing out their effect on the business model. The model represents the firm and its behaviour and generates reports on the outcome of alternatives. However, the model is only a model and is only as good as the assumptions and characteristics built into it. This fundamental rule must not be forgotten, otherwise model users are in danger of believing the model is true and reality is false!

The function of management reports is to inform management such that they are able to control their areas of responsibility. In expressing control, decisions will be made, resulting in feedback and corrective action to activities that are under-performing, and/or feed forward to review plans and implementations of future activity. In order to fulfil their function, management require decision supports and these are immediately available in the management reporting model into which proposed decisions may be placed and tested to evaluate the outcomes. This potential to "what if?" significantly improves the capabilities of management in controlling their activities and may be used both in the feedback to the activity or the feed forward to future plans.

In particular the role of management is based on the concepts of control within a system, which we first referred to in Chapter 1. Refer back to Figure 1.4, the planning and control loop.

Fundamental to the control loop is the information flow that commences with the implementation of the plans in the activity. The actual performance is measured in the output coming from the activity, e.g. orders received as a result of the salesman's visit. This information flow about actual activity is naturally historic, although real time systems are increasingly being implemented.

In order for this data to have real meaning, we must compare the output results with the input plans, and this is done in the comparison (review Figure 1.5 in Chapter 1). Information is distinguished from data in that it has a value to the receiver and leads to action. This can be seen in the comparison stage, where information generated from the comparison results in either feedback (corrective action to the activity through the amendment of the future flows) or feed forward (which leads to the revision of the plans and subsequent activities). Anthony (1965), suggested that these information flows of feedback and feed forward flowed up and down the planning hierarchy, from strategic plan-

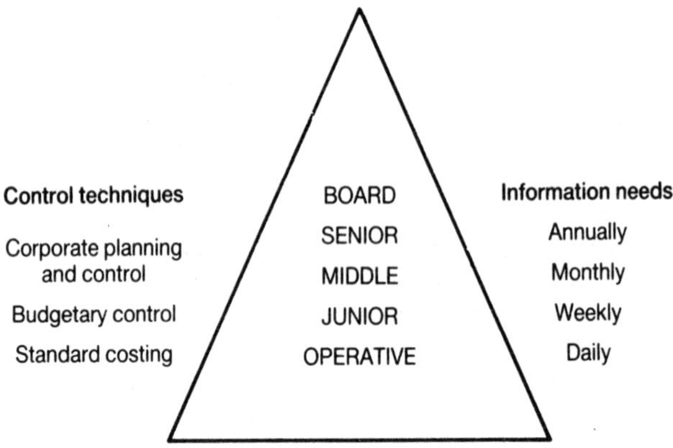

FIGURE 7.2 Anthony hierarchy, modified to show information flows

ning to management control, and operational control and then back again.

We can consider a top-down hierarchy that is chronological in its order. The corporate plan is for a specific five-year period that is prepared in an annual review process in which the last five-year plan is reviewed and replaced in part with the passage of time. It can be reviewed at any time, but the annual cycle fits with the fiscal year, the reporting year and the annual budget process.

At the next level we find the budget which, while annually prepared and linked to annual sales forecasting, is subject to review on a quarterly or more frequent basis. It is noteworthy at this point that some organizations now consider the budgeting process to be unnecessary, since through the use of financial modelling packages it is possible to reforecast and re-budget every month for the next twelve months. This has been described as "continuous business forecasting", which embodies the true philosophy of the budget process while exploiting modern financial planning techniques and computer technology.

The budget is the annual plan that is subject to quarterly or more frequent reviews. However, it is used as a control activity for each month and thus we have a monthly cycle as well. The monthly cycle not only considers the budget but also will attenuate the data from the daily and the weekly activities. The monthly activity predominantly compares the budget with the actual, to generate variances. The weekly activity and the daily activity are more likely to compare latest estimates and forecasts in critical control areas like sales and production, omitting the concepts of budgets but maybe including the concepts of standard costing. These weekly and daily activities tend to involve critical factors and the information is promptly available. In all cases the degree of detail available and its promptness is a function of the complexity of the critical factors, the size of the information processing system (whether manual or computerized) and the requirements of management.

Essentially the management accounting routines are cycles of forecasting, measuring and comparing, leading to reforecasting and reaction to variances. These routines are the natural base on which the computerization of management accounting and management information systems has evolved. It is only natural therefore that we should consider how organizations have achieved this in practice. The model that we have built is not an exhaustive model but rather an illustrative model of the principles involved. Our illustration has been centred on the monthly reporting activity to be found in many organizations, particularly those with departmental structure and divisionalization. In these organizations we are likely to find a budgeting process undertaken in an annual and quarterly review basis linked to a standard costing system, particularly in the processing industries. The actual data are likely to come from a computerized accounting information system that could either be a mini or mainframe or even micro-based system. This computerized accounting information system may well incorporate the budget data and generate simple variance reports. However, these reports are unlikely to be in an acceptable format for management and this is where the financial modelling package may be used to edit and filter the data into a more comprehensive and insightful report.

PLANNING

Planning is the process of *prevoyance*, forecasting future circumstances and planning to meet them. It consists of logistics (resource allocation) and strategy. It is a dynamic process that reflects continuity and flexibility; and though flexible, it is also, when required, precise. These characteristics are summarized in Drucker's (1974) definition of planning as:

> A continuous process of making present entrepreneurial decisions systematically and with best possible knowledge of their futurity, organizing systematically the effort needed to carry out these decisions, and measuring the results of these decisions against expectations through organized systematic feedback.

The notion of anticipating events has been developing since the turn of the century, but has assumed increasing urgency over the last thirty years. Until then, firms could rely with confidence on the use of historical data banks to extrapolate future trends. As the pace of change has accelerated, however, and as the environment has become more turbulent, responses have become more sophisticated. Table 7.1 shows the evolution of management systems since 1900.

In describing the overall decision process, Anthony (1965) offers a classification hierarchy that closely reflects the traditional pyramidal organization structure:

- *Strategic* The process, at an organization-wide level, of identifying objectives and changes in them, and the subsequent process of policy formulation, resource procurement, utilization and disposition, to achieve the stated objectives. Objectives give direction to the organization; policies indicate methodologies to be used. While not themselves necessarily long term, their consequences will be.
- *Management* The process by which managers implement policies by ensuring that resources are obtained, processed and disposed of effectively and efficiently in order to achieve organizational goals. It is the management who develop the operational capacity to meet the strategic objectives of the firm.
- *Operations* The process of effectively and efficiently implementing tasks and actions defined by management decisions so that management objectives may be achieved.

At the strategic level, business decisions are centred upon interactions with the environment. Changes in the environment create problems of uncertainty; decision making at this level tends therefore to include a greater element of risk and is often based on limited information. Such problems decrease as we descend the hierarchy, when decisions become progressively more structured, defined and based on fuller information.

On the basis of the classification set out in Table 7.2, computability and man-machine profiles can be shown as illustrated in Figure 7.3.

Table 7.2 illustrates principal decision classes. These classifications are incremental rather than descrete and they shift the emphasis from the operational "here and now" to the wider, longer-term perspective of the strategic. In so doing they mimic the shift in organizational spheres of responsibility in the hierarchy.

This, then, provides a structure within which business decisions can be taken. It is with long-term, strategic planning that we shall concern ourselves in this chapter.

PROBLEM SOLVING

The process of problem solving normally comprises four stages:

1. Recognition of the problem.
2. Search for courses of action which address the problem.

Table 7.1 Evolution of management systems.

Environment	*1900*	*1930*	*1950*	*1970*	*1990*
Future	*Stable*	*Reactive*	*Anticipating*	*Exploring*	*Creative*
Recurring	• systems and procedures manuals				
Forecasting by extrapolation		• financial control			
		• short-term budgeting			
			• capital budgeting		
			• management by objectives		
			• long-term planning		
Predictable threats and opportunities				• periodic strategic planning	
				• periodic strategic management	
				• issue analysis	
Partially predictable "weak signals"				• real time strategic management	
Unpredictable surprises					• surprise management

from Ansoff (1968): Planned Management of Turbulent Change.

Table 7.2 Classification of strategic planning, management and operation control.

Decisions	*Strategic planning*	*Management control*	*Operational control*
Problems	Selecting product mix. Selecting mix which optimizes return on investment of business	Optimization of resources	Optimizing ROI potential.
Nature of problem	Allocation of resources between products. Market opportunities.	Organization, acquisition and development of resources	Budgeting resources functions, scheduling, supervision and control.
Key decisions	Objectives and targets strategy. Diversification strategy. Expansion strategy. Admin. strategy. Finance of strategy. Growth strategy.	Organization, flows of information and work. Resource acquisition and development.	Operation targets and objects. Pricing, output, stock, research and development.
Key characteristics	Centralization of decision. Non-repetitive decisions. Partial ignorance. Non-self regeneration decisions.	Conflict between strategy and operations. Conflict of individuals. Economic and social link.	Decentralization. Risk and uncertainty. Large volume of decisions. Complexity. Decisions self-generative, deterministic.
e.g.:	Corporate planning and control	Budgetary control	Standard costing

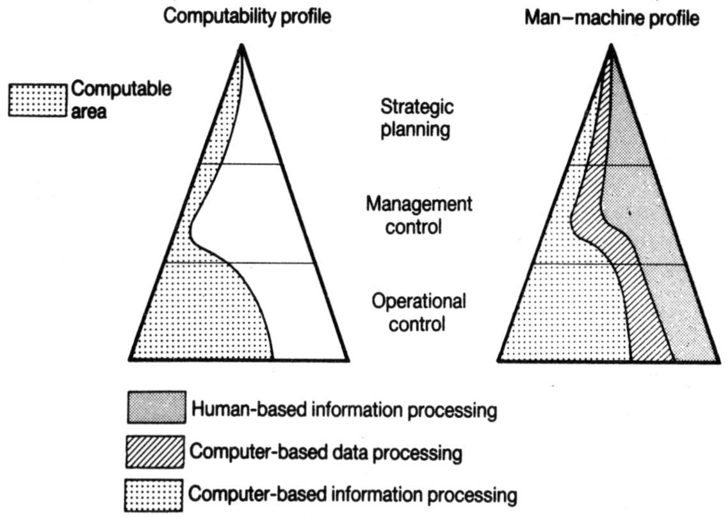

FIGURE 7.3 Computability and man-machine profiles

3. Evaluation of these alternatives.
4. Choice of one or more alternatives.

To these can be added control, whereby actual against planned results can be monitored, compared and contrasted.

Ansoff (1968), however, perceived a need for a method that would go further towards monitoring the business environment, coping with multiple conflicting objectives and identifying unique product-market opportunities. In formulating his "theory of strategic decisions", therefore, Ansoff requires that:

1. All of the four stages described above be included, with the emphasis on stages 1. and 2.
2. Resource allocations can be managed in the context of partial ignorance; i.e. allowing for as yet unknown opportunities, as well as those already evident.
3. Joint effects (synergy) arising from new activities be evaluated.
4. Opportunities with significant advantages can be marked out.
5. Provisions can be made for potentially conflicting objectives.
6. A long-term view of alternatives can be taken, notwithstanding the unreliability of cash flow projections.

The method that results is called the "Adaptive Search Method for Strategy Formulation". It employs a "cascade" approach, by which possible decision rules are expressed in broad terms to start with but are refined and made precise as the method proceeds. It involves three steps:

1. choosing whether or not to diversify;
2. selecting a broad product-market scope;
3. refining the scope.

Feedback is an important element. As Ansoff explains: "Since the cascade is a process of search for the solution, information may develop at later stages which casts doubt on previous decisions."

Within each of the three steps of the cascade, the approach is to:

1. establish objectives;
2. estimate the difference between the firm's current position and its objectives;
3. formulate alternative strategies;
4. evaluate the potential of each strategy to reduce the difference.

Thus both objectives and evaluation can be revised in line with new information as it arises. The emphasis in this approach lies in the continuous process of iteration. The steps are not necessarily carried out serially, but according to the information gained as each step is concluded. The need to systematize the approach for purposes of presentation frequently masks the principle of iteration.

OBJECTIVES

Throughout the previous section, frequent reference has been made to the term "objectives", and it is generally agreed that the first task in planning is to specify objectives.

Opinion varies considerably about the weight which attaches to different objectives. Drucker (1958), for instance, proposed that the main aim of a business was survival. Abrahams (1954), however, took account of social responsibility in suggesting that a firm must "maintain an equitable and working balance among the claims of the various directly interested groups – stockholders, employees, customers, and the public at large."

The introduction of an ethical element led to the "stakeholder" theory of objectives, in which the interests of all parties who are in some way connected with the firm – shareholders, employees, customers, the local community, etc. – should, it was believed, be represented. Argenti (1974) is sceptical about this, suggesting that the theory raises more questions than it answers. His view is that the sole objective is to generate return for shareholders, but only after the firm has discharged the obligations imposed by society and by its own ethos.

From the variety of theories put forward there has emerged a general view that firms have both economic and non-economic objectives, but that it is the economic objectives that are the principal determinant of a firm's activity. In turn, there is overall agreement that the main economic objective is profitability, though this is often constrained by the non-economic factors.

Taking profitability as the central objective, Ansoff sets out a number of subsidiary (or proxy) objectives that contribute to increasing the rate of return. The first is what he terms "proximate profitability", or the desired value of ROI over a three to ten-year period. But while attempting to achieve this, commitment to longer-term profitability (the long-term objective) through the allocation of resources for research and development, new plant and equipment, etc. must be made. As the time horizon increases, however, forecasting and measuring ROI become more difficult and he suggests that a more accurate measure might be found by the evaluation of key characteristics that contribute towards profitability. In terms of its competitive position, for example, sales, market share and increasing product ranges will be important indicators. The secondary objective of internal efficiency, expressed in terms of turnover ratios, personnel skills and modern physical assets, are of equal importance. The third subsidiary objective is flexibility – the ability of the firm to respond to unforeseen events. External flexibility includes both defensive and aggressive policies; internal flexibility is reflected in liquidity or resources. Figure 7.4 illustrates the hierarchy of the long-term objective and Figure 7.5 that of the flexibility of objective. Figure 7.6 gives an overview of the process of setting objectives and includes reference to appraisal that we discuss below.

APPRAISAL

Having established its objectives, the next step is for the organization to survey its present state; it does so by carrying out internal and external appraisals.

Internal appraisal

The process of internal appraisal is used to identify a company's strengths and weaknesses and is a vital step in establishing its level of competence in the area in which it operates. Argenti (1974) proposes that the following fields should be covered:

- financial;
- productive;

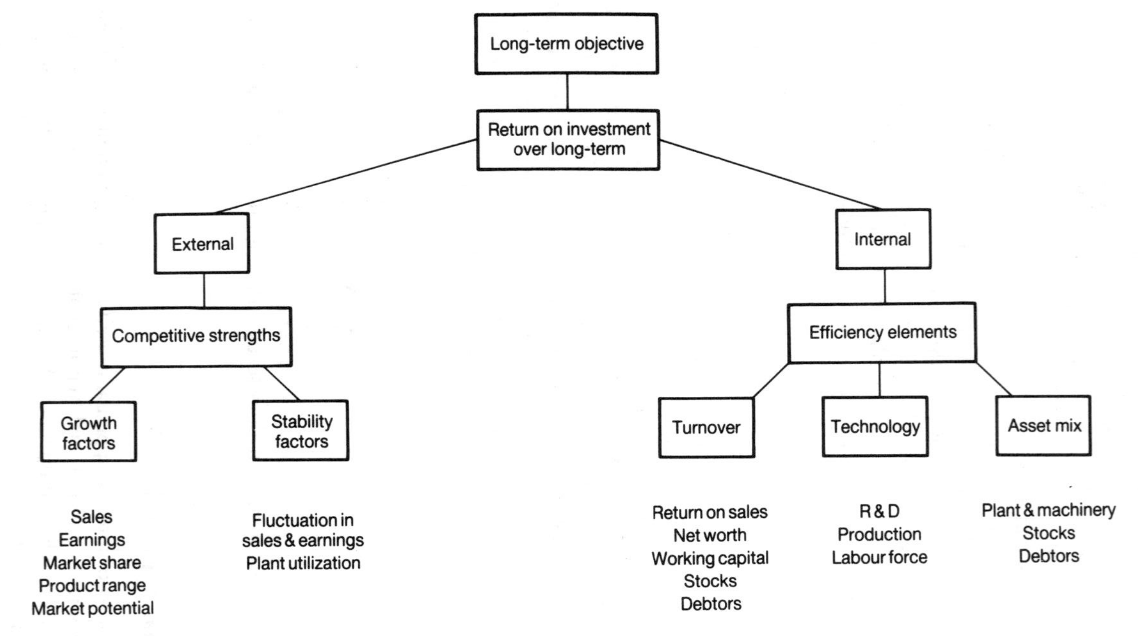

FIGURE 7.4 Hierarchy of long-term objective

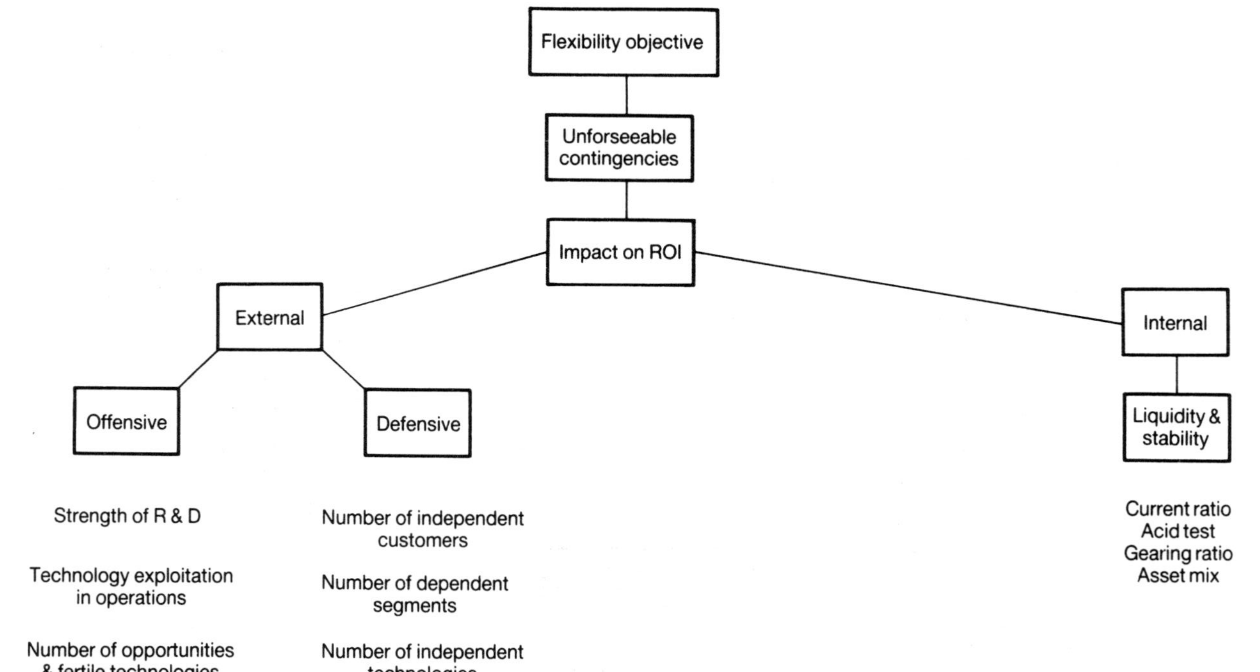

FIGURE 7.5 Flexibility of objective

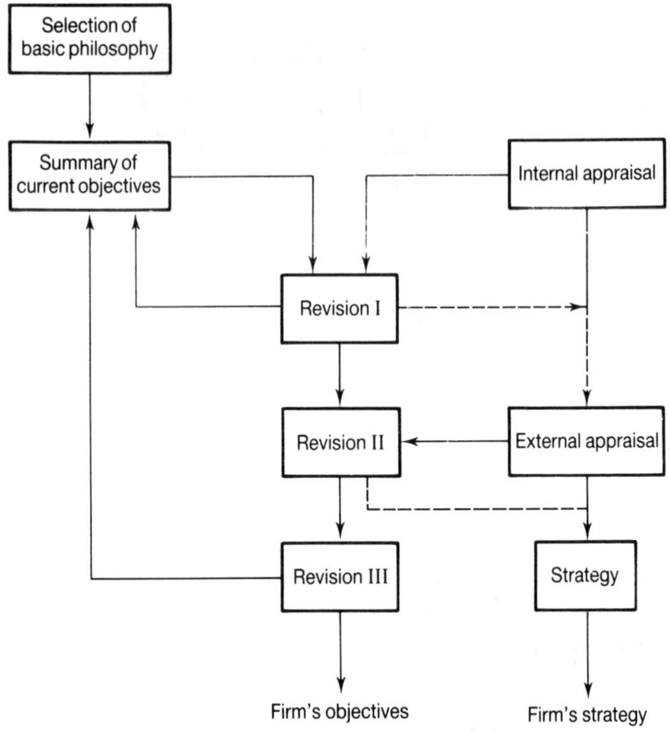

FIGURE 7.6 Objective-setting

- marketing and distribution;
- buying;
- research;
- employees;
- management;
- position in industry.

A starting point will be to compare past with current performance and to extrapolate future trends. For purposes of comparison, competitors' financial reports will also be useful sources. Further information can be obtained from such systems as Data Stream, Dun and Bradstreet's on-line and Prestel's Citipages that provide current financial data; historical data are available through Microexstat. Marketing information can be found in the trade press and Nielsen and AGB reports. Details about the industrial sector are obtainable from the Intercompany Comparison Service and from trade associations.

As this internal exercise proceeds, an analysis should simultaneously be carried out of the relevant industrial sector to establish overall economic and competitive prospects.

Synergy

Closely allied to the identification of strengths and weakness is the concept of synergy. It is often referred to in the literature as the "2 + 2 = 5 effect", to indicate that a company can generate a combined return on resources greater than the sum of its parts. Synergy is the "fit" between a company's current product market position and another into which it may wish to move. In making this move it will look for opportunities that will take advantage of its strengths and will provide increased efficiency in areas of weakness. Synergy can be identified in a number of areas such as management, distribution and production, and can occur either in the initial stages of an activity or during operation.

External appraisal

External appraisal, also known as environmental analysis, is directed towards the identification of opportunities and threats and involves a survey of all factors that might impact on the firm, including governmental and societal influences as well as those from the industry itself. Higgins (1980) tabulates major categories of external information, as shown in Table 7.3. Much of the knowledge required to carry out external appraisal can be obtained from market research organizations and investment analysts, who maintain comprehensive environmental monitoring systems.

Performance gap analysis

At the end of the appraisal stage, sufficient information should be available to enable the company to make forecasts of future performance, based on the assumption that it will react to new events as it has to past events. Comparing these forecasts with the objectives previously arrived at will lead to two different sets of figures. This is known as the performance gap. Figure 7.7 taken from Higgins highlights the way in which the gap can be used to indicate if and when new strategies will be required; it also illustrates both the size and time horizons of the task. Gap analysis is a valuable tool in helping to determine whether existing plans are

Table 7.3 Major categories of external information.

Main information category	*Sub-categories*
Microeconomic environment	
(i) government policy and national/international influences	(i) Overall economic indicators e.g. GNP growth and inflation rates; economic policies, e.g., taxation, grants aids
(ii) the industry	(ii) Numbers of companies, their sizes and performance, e.g. output and profitability; competitors' investment plans
Socio-political environment	
(i) legislation and government and political attitudes	(i) legislation on employment, health and safety, etc.
(ii) attitudes of society	(ii) Consumerism, attitudes to work and profit, environmentalism, etc.
The market-place	Product } own and Price } competition Distribution channels and buyer behaviour adjusting and promotion
The technological characteristics of the industry	Rate of research, development and innovation, both within company and industry, at the product and process levels

sufficient, or whether alternative courses of action are going to be required.

EVALUATION

At the end of the appraisal process it is probable that a company will be faced with a whole gamut of possible strategies and some form of evaluation and elimination will therefore be required. In the context of a corporate plan, the aim is to identify an overall strategic structure, and to this end six central questions must be addressed. Does the proposed strategy:

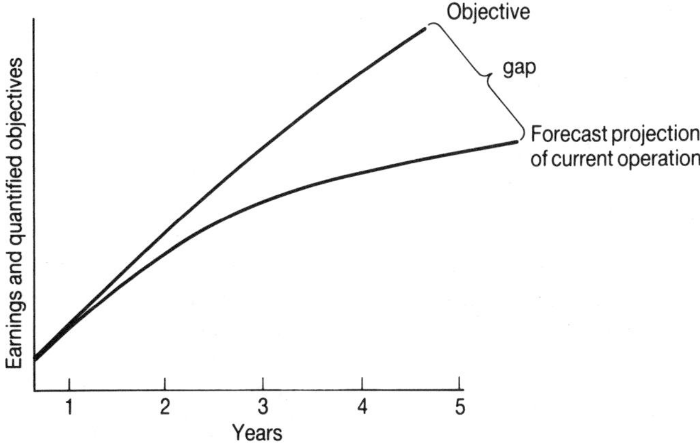

(i) Divergence which progressively widens, requiring action in the medium term

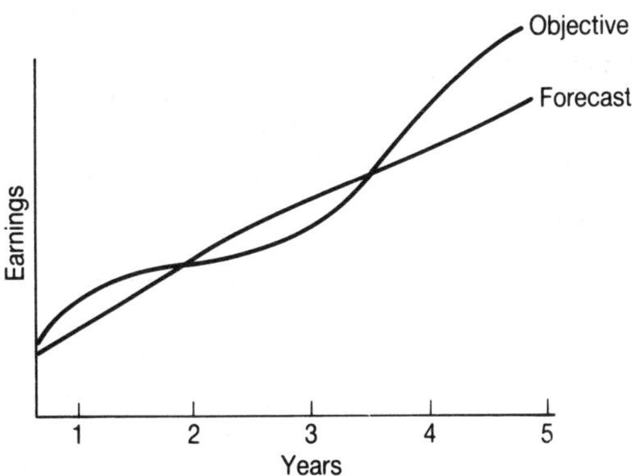

(ii) No immediate problems, but need to monitor towards the end of Year 4

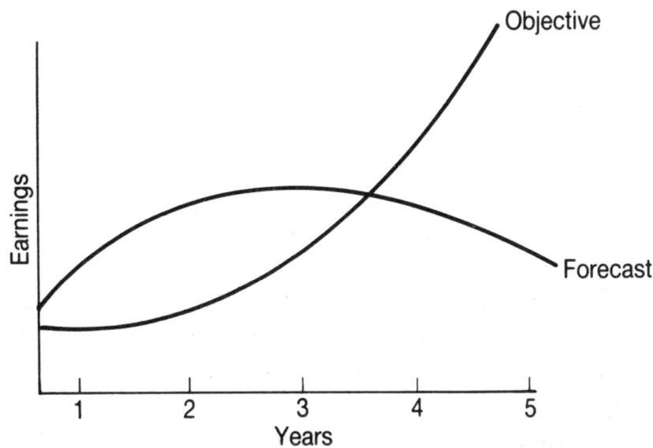

(iii) Problem appearing in Year 3 which is serious by Year 5. Need for new strategy

FIGURE 7.7 Performance gap illustrations

- build on the company's strengths?
- correct or reduce principal weaknesses?
- exploit future opportunities?
- mitigate present or future threats?
- create confidence (i.e. is it feasible)?
- meet non-economic objectives (i.e. is it acceptable)?

These issues can only be dealt with if there is a clear understanding about three further questions. These are:

- What businesses are we in?
- What is the relationship between our existing businesses?
- What are the new directions we are contemplating?

To assist in analysing these matters, Ansoff constructed a matrix of growth vector components (Table 7.4) which shows the company's future direction relative to its current product market stance. (In this context, Ansoff defined "mission" as an existing product need.)

Further assistance can be gained from using a product portfolio matrix (Table 7.5), in which characteristics of product groups are analysed according to their cash demands and cash-generating capabilities.

Table 7.4 Product-mission matrix.

Product / **Mission**	*Present*	*New*
Present	Market penetration	Product development
New	Market development	Diversification

Table 7.5 Product portfolio matrix.

	Cash generation		
Cash use	Problem child (Do something to stop it)	Star (Watch it)	*High*
	Dog (Kick it)	Cash cow (Milk it)	*Low*
	Low	*High*	

Possible strategies can also be identified from life cycle analysis, also known as the S-curve (Figure 7.8) whose characteristics – birth, fast growth, maturity/stability, decline – can be applied to most products, markets and companies.

Whatever techniques are used to assist with evaluation and identification of strategies, planners must remember constantly to refer back to the objectives established during the first stage, and to measure each of the strategies against the proximate, long-term and flexibility criteria.

The use of the sorts of aids mentioned above will help reduce the number of alternative strategies to a realistic level and in many cases a company will be faced with a choice between expansion and diversification. In Ansoff's terms, expansion means increased market penetration and the development of new products and markets. He contends that since diversification entails higher costs and risks, and because synergy will be greater in expansion, firms should first establish whether they can achieve their objectives without diversifying. A major factor in considering expansion will be what has emerged during the internal appraisal of strengths and weaknesses and how a company measures up against successful competitors in the same market. Equally, the analysis of industry potential, including indications of growth, profitability and market share, will be vital. Non-achievement of objectives through expansion is, according to Ansoff, one of four situations that will lead firms to diversify. The others are:

1. When the retained cash exceeds the total expansion needs.
2. When, even if the present product market is expanded, greater profitability can be achieved outside it.
3. When there is insufficient information to provide a reliable comparison between diversification and expansion.

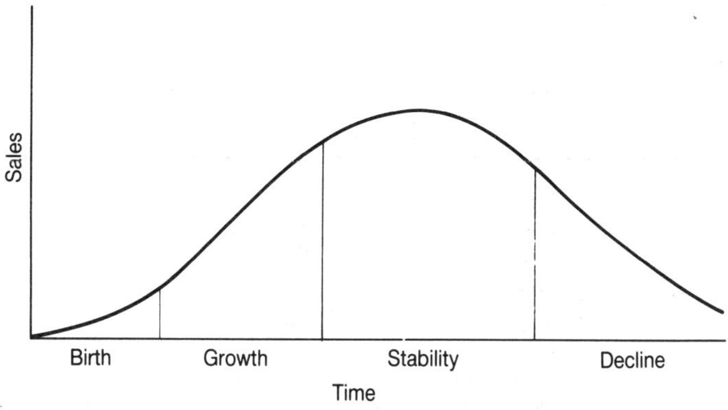

FIGURE 7.8 Product life cycle

The final stage of evaluation will involve an in-depth financial analysis of the short-listed strategies. It is in this process that the use of computer-based models will be of value.

SCENARIO PLANNING

Scenario planning is a means of modelling the future. Taking the current state of the business and building in certain assumptions about the environment, a projected position is formulated. By using a dynamic model it is then possible to demonstrate the impact of these assumptions on the organization's future performance. We also referred to the fact that the use of unrealistic assumptions had led to scenario planning becoming discredited. The need for proportion is summarized by Argenti (1974) thus: "The key to a good scenario is that it should describe a *feasible* sequence of events that are consistent with each other and with the relevant features of the real world."

Internal and external options

In constructing a scenario, a variety of internal and external options may be considered which will encompass both qualitative and quantitative factors. Examples of internal options include:

- increasing or reducing the work-force;
- adding to or deleting from the product range;
- changing products;
- expanding or contracting production facilities;
- changing production technology;
- changing advertising;
- changing distribution and marketing methods;
- moving into new markets.

Some or all of these may be combined to form a scenario. It might be decided, for instance, to combine new markets, new products, new production facilities and new marketing to produce a particular scenario. Another scenario might be to take no action. Both can then be processed using a dynamic model and the results of each compared with a number of criteria, in particular the corporate objectives to which we referred in the previous section.

Also to be considered are external options. A variable such as sales volume, for example, is not entirely independent of assumptions about pricing and advertising/marketing expenditure. However, given a situation in which prices are determined and in which there already exists a pricing/advertising budget, the sales volume may very well be a function of factors and variables that are normally outside the company's control. These include exchange rates, inflation rates, interest rates and wage rates. Exchange rate movement, for instance, an area in which some fairly drastic developments have occurred in the past few years, can completely eliminate the profits of one market and open up competitive new opportunities in another part of the world. Similarly, wage rates are not entirely independent of production and capacity utilization rates, to the extent that low wage rates can impact adversely on industrial relations. So the overlap and mutuality of external and internal factors must constantly be borne in mind.

Complexity versus simplicity

An important consideration when building a model is the number of variables to be used. On the whole, the greater the number, the more realistic the model is likely to be. Equally, a simpler model is an easier vehicle for experimentation as the number of variables and assumptions are smaller and more easily remembered, and their impact more readily understood.

Number of scenarios

Taking account of external and internal factors, any number of scenarios can be drawn up for any given company. Some limit is clearly needed and for planning purposes the norm is three (although in some situations only two are used, in order to force a choice). Where three scenarios are used, they can be presented in terms of high, medium and low achievement. In these circumstances, however, there is a tendency always to choose the middle way. The more accepted approach is to project the so-called "surprise-free", i.e. expected scenario, for comparison with two alternatives respectively representing better than expected and worse than expected outcomes.

CONTROL

We have so far described the stages involved in arriving at a corporate plan and the sequence in which they arise. The completion of these steps is not, however, the end of the exercise; planning is a continuous process and involves the company in what Argenti calls "monitoring confidence". A corporate plan is chosen because there is confidence that it will reduce the gap between objectives and forecasts. But the factors that contributed towards the choice of strategy – strengths, weaknesses, opportunities and threats – are not static, they will change over time as a result of internal or external factors, or both. If suitable responses are not forthcoming, or if planned actions are not taken, confidence will be lost. Argenti sums up as follows:

> The confidence that managers feel in a given strategy is less dependent upon actual results than upon the company successfully taking those actions prescribed in the plan and on their confidence in the continuing validity of the assumptions, forecasts, opinions, etc. that went into their original strategic decision.

Discrepancies between planned and actual performance can arise for a variety of reasons. Intelligent use of a computer model, however, should enable ready identification of some of the underlying causes of variances. Here too, though, confidence is a factor. In 1974, Grinyer and Wooller conducted a survey of the use of computer-based financial models and found six main reasons connected with the success of a financial modelling exercise:

1. Sponsorship and continued support were given by top management.
2. Top management understood and had confidence in the model, and were prepared to place at least some reliance on forecast results.
3. The model met specific management decision-making needs.
4. The data required as input were readily available and not voluminous.
5. The model was embedded in the planning process (i.e. was used as a matter of course during normal planning procedures).
6. The model was properly documented throughout its development.

Failure tended to result if any three of these conditions were not present. It is our opinion that their findings would not be equally relevant today, partly because of the micro revolution. Grinyer and Wooller were talking of an era when models took a great deal of manpower and mainframe resources. Today modelling is more an extension of the desk calculator. Nevertheless, their points are still pertinent.

What to control

Having identified that there is a routine reporting cycle, this reporting cycle is primarily focused on control of critical factors. It is therefore essential to identify the success factors or key points that must be considered in an organization. Once these factors have been identified, then consideration may be given to reporting them that may be in a dynamic form or a static form. A dynamic model will best be achieved through regular reporting showing trends and cycles, and the static by periodic reports comparing status at those points.

Type of control	Type of centre	Measure of performance	Problems
Overall financial control	Investment	Return on capital employed	Only measures economic performance; assumes profit maximization but corporate goals may be cash generation, market share, etc.
Short term	Profit centre	Profit margin either as percentage on sales or an absolute	Profit may be maximized in short term at a cost to long-term capital maintenance
		Alternative residual income after charge for cost of capital.	Overcomes some problems of disinvestment for short-term profit
Functional	Revenue centre	Sales revenue by outlet, product and customer	Strictly limited as sales performance is not solely dependent on sales activity but also on competitors' economic and social outlook etc.
	Cost centre	Cost classified by elements and behaviour	Perhaps the most strictly controlled but should be seen as related to volumes and fixed charges

FIGURE 7.9 Control philosophy and measures of performance

Fundamentally we may consider that profit is our objective as expressed within the return on the capital employed. Critical to this, therefore, will be what the profit is, how it has been achieved, where it has been achieved, and what capital has been employed in order to achieve this. Profit is generated from the sale of goods at a minimum cost. Therefore if we wish to maximize the profit, we must maximize our sales revenue and minimize our costs. This control of sales, debtors, cash flow, production costs and expenditure is a critical element in our success. How can this be measured within an organization? In one recent case study control of these elements was achieved as follows:

> Sales were measured by outlets while costs were measured by product groups, i.e. the products that incurred the costs, plus the expenses of departments. Capital employed was measured through two routes: one by ratios, and secondly by consideration of specific working capital items that were critical to the success, e.g. stocks, and debtors. Control over the production process was also identified specifically through the product groups and expenses but in addition items such as staffing and overtime and energy were separately identified. Lastly cash flow was considered since this was the essential liquid to maintain the organization. Where organizations are multi-divisional and there is inter-company trading, control of inter-divisional performance will be necessary through consideration of that trading activity.

Management accounts will emphasize those critical items in their reporting, by producing specific schedules, graphs and tables associated with critical success factors. These tables will predominantly identify the variances associated with the trends, cycles and the abnormalities, and through variance analysis the symptoms or sources may be established. Through a process of decomposing the variances into their elements, (e.g. sales – a poor performance in the sales revenue may be associated not only with price but also with volume and the mix of products sold) the cause of the abnormalities may be identified and corrective action taken. Thus the separation of those variances into product and outlet will help identify the cause of any problem in sales to customers, packs or mixes of sales.

MANAGEMENT ACCOUNTING AND PERIODIC REPORTING

The first question that must be addressed is why we looked at management accounting and periodic reporting, when we are considering financial planning? The answer is that the financial planning tools that we use can be applied to routine reporting. One of their major characteristics is their ability to present data in a format that is easily digestible by the reader and is pleasant to read in its format. In addition, financial modelling packages are capable of handling large volumes of data, compressing them through attenuation (subtotalling quickly) and thus satisfying routine reporting requirements of management. Routine reporting usually means large volumes of data must be handled very rapidly if the value of the information is to be maintained. At the same time, financial modelling permits management accounting reports to be produced in a fuller manner than has traditionally been possible.

The function of management reports is to inform management such that they are able to control their areas of responsibility. In expressing control, decisions will be made resulting in feedback and corrective action to activities that are under-performing, and/or feed forward to review to plans and implementations of future activity. In order to fulfil this function, management require decision supports, and these are immediately available in the management reporting model into which proposed decisions may be placed and tested to evaluate the outcomes. This potential of "what if?"ing significantly improves the capabilities of management in controlling their activities and may be used both in the feedback to the activity or feed forward to future plans.

For this reason we also considered the use of integrated modelling packages as applied to management accounting and periodic reporting. We believe that these integrated systems offer significant features that may assist the practising accountant in generating better and more prompt reports to their management users. This is achieved through the nature of integrated systems that provide not only financial modelling facilities but also associated data bases, word processing and graphics. Thus the data bases may be used for storage of data such as budgets and standards as well as cumulative data; the word processors may be used for the editing and formatting of the printed report and the graphics facility permits the generation of management graphs, pie charts, and block or line graphs.

Executive information systems

An executive information system may be defined as a support for executive decision makers. It embodies decision support systems in a particular user-friendly manner. The key feature is the ability to provide a top perspective on the firm, linking detailed internal performance to external comparative performance of the firm against its competitors and the market-place. While the ability to incorporate detailed reports to support overview is little different from the traditional management reporting systems, the external comparative data have been hard to obtain and automatically incorporate, and many systems lack this facility. It is desirable to provide for both qualitative and quantitative data that can be problematic for data processing systems and disciplines such as accountancy with its emphasis on tangibility. Historic data should be readily available but timeliness has been a problem in some organizations. Predictive or forecast data have either to be entered or generated and automatic systems may be guilty of over-simplification, while the incorporation of user modelling implies modelling skills on the part of end users.

The experience and caution of traditional modellers are likely to lead to testing, anchoring and reconciling of reports before acceptance that an inexperienced user is unlikely to follow. Consequently there is an increased chance that the inexperts, when supported by powerful tools, can mislead themselves. It is therefore vital that end users approach such systems with caution and have the support and advice of an experienced modeller, while the system should incorporate learning support. The incorporation of expertise in these systems is increasingly common, but can only be in restricted areas due to the complexity of rules and logic that have to be incorporated. Exploiting the latest developments in the areas of expert systems, artificial intelligence, neural networks and Smart systems offers windows of opportunity, but should not be seen as a replacement for the detailed knowledge required by an executive or that acquired by modelling development.

The design specifications given by executives have failed to be met by most systems to date, but many organizations are aspiring to deliver some or all of the features of EIS, e.g. PILOT, METAPRAXIS, COMMANDER. The ability to support executives with structured internal data presented in a user-friendly manner is not problematic. However, the problem of external data is complicated by defining what are relevant data, and defining sources of data.

SUMMARY

Currently, managers do not have a comprehensive DSS available to them, but they may assemble a personalized system based on decision skills and situations. When building such systems they must take care to ensure the compatibility of systems so that data that is stored and processed in one system may be imported to another. In this way, raw data may be taken from the mainframe and, using some statistical package that permits identification of relationships, processed on the micro. Having established the model relationships, these can then be built into the model and the resulting decision returned to the mainframe as target or budgeted activity levels.

We would encourage managers to employ a variety of systems appropriate to the situation together with their own skills. Long-dormant expertise in mathematics and statistics, subjects that underpin much of this area, may be reawakened, particularly in relation to the new user-friendly mathematics processors and statistics packages that guide the user through the intricacies and overcome mundane number-crunching. An added bonus is that these packages can produce results in the form of graphical output, providing less experienced users with easily comprehended information. Recommending the use of the right system does, of course, assume a knowledge of what systems are on the market and what those systems offer. In talking to managers at all levels, we are constantly surprised at how little is known about the availability of even quite elementary tools.

References and further reading

Abrahams, F. (1954) "Management Responsibility in a Complex World", in T.H. Carrol (ed.), *Business Education for Competence and Responsibility*, University of North Carolina.

Alter, S.A. (1977) "A Taxonomy of decision support systems", *Sloan Management Review*, 19, No. 1, pp. 39–56.

Ansoff, H.I. (1968) *Corporate Strategy*, London: Penguin.

Anthony, R.N. (1965) *Planning and Control Systems: Framework for Analysis*, Cambridge, Mass.: Harvard University Press.

Argenti. (1974) *Systematic Corporate Planning*, Walton-on-Thames: Nelson.

Bowman, C. and Asch, D. (1987) *Strategic Management*, Basingstoke: Macmillan Education.

Bryant, J.W. (1987) *Financial Modelling in Corporate Management*, Chichester: Wiley.

Collier, P.A. (1984) *The Impact of Information Technology on the Management Accountant*, London: ICMA.

Drucker, P.F. (1958) "Business objectives and survival needs: notes on a discipline of Business Enterprise", *Journal of Business*, 31(2), pp. 81–90.

Drucker, P.F. (1974) *Management, Tasks, Responsibilities, Practices*, London: Harper & Row.

Gilligan, C., Neale, B. and Murray, D. (1983) *Business Decision Making*, Hemel Hempstead: Philip Allan.

Grinyer, P.H. and Wooller, J. (1978) *Corporate Models Today*, London: ICAEW.

Higgins, J.C. (1980) *Strategic and Operational Planning Systems – Principles and Practice*, Hemel Hempstead: Prentice Hall.

Holtham, C. (1992) *Executive Information Systems and Decision Support*, London: Chapman & Hall.

Keen, P.G.W. and Scott Morton, M.S. (1978) *Decision Support Systems: An Organisational Perspective*, Wokingham: Addison Wesley.

McCosh, A., Rahman, M. and Earl, M.J. (1981) *Developing Managerial Information Systems*, Basingstoke: Macmillan.

Plane, D.R. (1986) *Quantitative tools for decision support using IFPS*, Wokingham: Addison Wesley.

Rapport, A. (1982) *Information for Decision Making – Readings*, Hemel Hempstead: Prentice Hall.

Index